LEADER'S GUIDE

Who Am I?

15 SMALL GROUP STUDIES
ON DISCOVERING PERSONAL WORTH

DISCOVERY SERIES

ANNE DINNAN
LAUREL EDISON
KELLY D. PEAVEY

David C. Cook Church Ministries—Resources
A division of Cook Communications Ministries
Colorado Springs, CO/Paris, Ontario

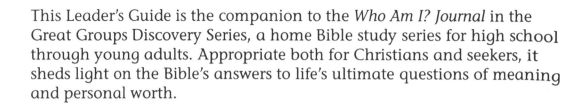

This Leader's Guide is the companion to the *Who Am I? Journal* in the Great Groups Discovery Series, a home Bible study series for high school through young adults. Appropriate both for Christians and seekers, it sheds light on the Bible's answers to life's ultimate questions of meaning and personal worth.

GREAT GROUPS
Discovery Series
Who Am I? Leader's Guide
© 1994 David C. Cook Publishing Co.

David C. Cook Church Ministries—Resources
A division of Cook Communications Ministries
4050 Lee Vance View; Colorado Springs, CO 80918-7100
Cable address: DCCOOK
Series editor: Anne Dinnan
Contributors: Anne Dinnan, David and Alyce T. Reimer, Kelly D. Peavey
Designer: Jeff Sharpton, PAZ Design Group
Cover illustrator: Ken Cuffe
Inside illustrator: Jim Carson
Printed in U.S.A.
ISBN: 0-7814-5133-7

TABLE OF Contents

Schedule

Meeting	Date	Location	Leaders	Helpers (food, etc.)
Optional Meeting				
Do I Matter?				
1				
2				
3				
4				
5				
One of a Kind				
6				
7				
8				
9				
10				
I'm Not Alone				
11				
12				
13				
14				
15				

Great Stuff about Great Groups!

Welcome to Great Groups—a new concept in youth ministry resources from David C. Cook. Great Groups is a three-tiered series of studies created for high schoolers and young adults who are at various stages of spiritual development. The three tiers—designed to move young people from being casual about Christianity to becoming committed followers of Jesus Christ—look like this:

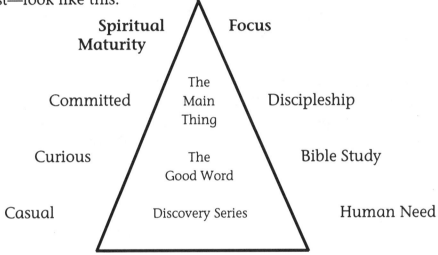

Spiritual Maturity

Focus

Committed — The Main Thing — Discipleship

Curious — The Good Word — Bible Study

Casual — Discovery Series — Human Need

Great Groups was created because:

- Not all young people are at the same stage of spiritual development;
- Intentional ministry is needed to guide people toward greater spiritual commitment;
- Real life change is possible through studying the Bible individually and discussing it together in small groups;
- Many young people are ready to lead discussion groups, so these studies encourage peer leadership;
- No two small groups are the same, so these studies pay attention to group dynamics.

Discovery Series—entry-level studies for seekers and those who've grown up in the church, but who may not have a complete understanding of what it means to be a Christian. These studies help people discover who they are from God's perspective and the difference that can make in every area of their lives. The Discovery Series assumes group members have little or no Bible background. Minimal advance preparation needed.

The Good Word—inductive studies for those who are curious about what the Bible really says. These studies help young people develop lifelong Bible study skills that will challenge them to feed themselves from Scripture. The Good Word series assumes group members have little or some Bible background. Moderate advance preparation needed.

The Main Thing—discipleship studies for those who want to be followers of Jesus Christ. These studies will challenge group members to take their faith seriously. The Main Thing series assumes group members have some or extensive Bible background. Thorough advance preparation needed.

Introduction:

Who Am I?

Suffering artist? Misunderstood genius? Budding star? Accident? Failure? Fake? Child of God? Masterpiece of Creation? Indispensable part of the body of Christ?

According to psychologist Erik Erikson, coming to a healthy and balanced sense of who you are is the most critical task of people moving into adulthood. It's crucial to being able to both love and work. Without it a person becomes either overly dependent, or unable to commit to anyone. A healthy sense of identity is a prerequisite to intimacy. It's also critical to finding your calling, your niche in life.

But this search for identity cannot be undertaken in a vacuum. We belong to each other. We need each other. That's why these Bible studies are about more than simply, "what do you believe?" The question "Who am I?" has to do with finding your significance, your uniqueness, and your place in relationship with others.

This series for small groups is specifically geared to seekers as well as Christians who want serious answers to their questions about themselves, God, and their place in this world. In these next fifteen studies, you will explore those aspects of identity together. Our hope is that you and your group members, whether Christians or not, will come to a stronger sense of self, and we pray, a true and living faith in the God who loves you as you are.

Acknowledgment

I've enjoyed developing this series and working with writers who understand the issues we all go through in that difficult transition from adolescence to full adulthood. Some of them are still in the thick of it themselves, which makes this series even more exciting. Thanks to all who contributed, not only through writing, but also by brainstorming ideas, reading the first drafts, and offering feedback on others' ideas.

Special thanks to my friend and prayer partner, Alyce T. who taught me so much about journaling, and ministering with searching young adults like our friend "Little Flower" who still has not come to believe that she matters to God. —Anne Dinnan, Editor.

How to Use This Material

Why a small group Bible study?

"No man is an island" said English poet John Donne. The search for identity is a personal search, but the irony is that it can never be discovered only on one's own. That is the reason for exploring the question in a small group setting. In your journal you can explore your own thinking, reflect and express your thoughts and feelings, always with reference to something greater than yourself, the Word of God. The small group should be a safe place to explore those things with others. In a sense, when you express something personal in a group, you do a reality check. The group either affirms or corrects your impression by their reactions, and you do the same for them. Sometimes that's painful, sometimes it's wonderfully affirming. The important thing is to be sensitive, to respect and listen to one another, and to be gentle with one another.

Throughout this guide, there will be suggestions for activity ideas and questions to help build a sense of community in which true discovery can take place.

Digging In: Studying the Bible Inductively

You do not have to *believe* the Bible to study it inductively. All that's required is an openness to letting the text speak for itself. Inductive means you go from the particular, in this case the text in front of you, to the general—what you can learn from it.

The role of the leader in an inductive study is to ask questions and guide the group members into the text to *dig out* the meaning for themselves, rather than *telling* them what it means. The leader is not the expert. In fact, anyone can lead.

Studying the Bible requires adherence to the same rules of interpretation you would use in interpreting any body of literature. But first, a ground rule: The text is the authority, not something you heard in a sermon or what some book says (though these can be helpful). Stick to the passage under discussion and let it speak for itself.

Here are the three basic guidelines of interpretation:

1. What does the passage say? (Observation) Answering this involves the 5 Ws and 1 H of journalism:

• *Who* is writing or speaking, and to whom? *Who* are the people involved?

• *What* kind of writing is it? (Letter, poem, historical account, narrative, prophecy). *What* parts can we see? *What* was the writer's train of thought? *What* are the author's tactics? *What* is happening?

• *Where* is the action taking place? (What country, or at whose house, and what does the setting tell you?)

• *When* is all this happening? (This does not mean just a date or year unless the text says so. It means at what point in Jesus' ministry. Or, after what and before what other events in the Bible. Or, at what time of day—whatever the text itself says about time.)

• *Why?* Does one event or person cause something else to happen? *What* are the motives and feelings here? *Why* did the author write this? Is he persuading, reporting, worshiping, teaching, etc.

• *How* does each part relate to the whole? *How* is the story or argument being told or arranged?

2. What does it mean? (Interpretation) Only when you've analyzed the text to find out what it actually says can you answer the question, what does it mean? This is where most problems of interpretation come in. Sometimes there are layers of meaning, but usually there is one basic meaning of the text, at least for the times in which it was written. This, of course, does not mean that you will like what it says, but if the text is allowed to speak for itself, rather than having us impose the meaning we want on it, we can accept or reject it with integrity.

To discover the meaning of the text, ask questions such as this: how does the style affect our interpretation? Did the writer intend for this to be taken literally, or is it a story with a moral to it, such as the parables of Jesus? There are legitimate differences of interpretation on some passages, but discovering the writer's intent eliminates many, if not most different meanings.

3. What does it mean to me? (Application) Too often people jump right to to this question the first time they read a passage. In fact, this is the last question you should answer. Only when the first two questions are answered can you legitimately ask what the passage means to you specifically, and to people in general.

The Holy Spirit is ultimately the interpreter of His Word to our hearts, and you don't have to be a scholar to understand and "hear" God speaking to you through a verse or passage of Scripture. But by jumping to this question without really understanding what the text actually says and what it means, you can come up with errors and weird interpretations.

Sharing the Leadership

This series is designed to be led by participants. The leader doesn't have to be an expert (the text is, remember?). Most sessions have leadership tips to help you in your role as leader. Basically, the leader's role is to ask questions and guide the group in discovery. You might want to rotate the leadership so that everyone has a chance to lead. If some people don't want to lead a study, that's okay. Start off with someone who's led a Bible study before, go for a few weeks, and then hand off the leadership to someone else.

The leader's job is to facilitate discussion. Do not allow anyone—not even yourself—to monopolize the discussion. Try to draw out more reserved members, but don't force anyone to talk who doesn't want to. Give people time to think and don't be afraid of a little silence.

If someone comes up with an "off the wall" interpretation, ask something like, "Where do you see that meaning in the text?" Sometimes the group corrects itself. Someone might wonder about the comment and say what he or she sees in the verses. Or you could ask other people what they think—as long as they stick with the text too.

If someone brings up something that's off the subject of the text, say so, but offer to follow up on it later. Don't let the group get sidetracked into an argument. If there's a legitimate disagreement, let people express their points, and then say, "Let's move on; we can discuss this later," or even, "we probably have to agree to disagree about this, but let's continue with the study."

What version of the Bible should we use?

This really doesn't matter, but whatever you use, it's a good idea for everyone to use the same version of the Scripture. You may want to have an alternate translation along for comparison purposes, but it avoids confusion if everyone is reading the same text. Another value in using the same translation (in the same edition) is that you can tell people what page to turn to for those who don't yet know how to find things in the Bible.

Most of the Scripture printed in the journal is in the NIV. This is a good modern translation. If you want to use the NIV, you can order inexpensive paperback versions from the International Bible Society.

The Format

These studies are broken down into three five-week units. As a group, decide how you will approach this material. These units build on each other, of course, so it's ideal if you have fifteen weeks to go through them all in order, with perhaps a break in between. Do at least make an initial five-week commitment, and then you can reevaluate.

Another group decision is how much time you'll spend together for each group study. The study can easily be done in an hour to an hour and a half. Two hours together will give you time for refreshments afterward. Be sure to allow at least 30 minutes for the study itself and 5-10 minutes for actual prayer at the end, not just sharing requests. Also, make sure it's understood exactly when your study is going to start, and always start at the same time to ensure commitment. Here's an outline of the format with suggested time limits for each part.

1 Getting Started (15-20 minutes)

One of the most important parts of your time together. You can use this time to welcome new people, help people get to know each other, and move into a frame of mind to discuss the topic of the week.

Housekeeping (3-5 minutes)

This is the place for announcements (for example, a change in the meeting location, a schedule change, or plans for a social activity outside of group time). Keep these short and sweet.

Icebreaker (5-10 minutes)

A mixer, getting-to-know-you type activity to help people feel that the group is a safe place for sharing non-threatening things.

Opening (5 minutes)

This is a transition activity to open yourselves to God and invite His Presence with you through singing, prayer, or other creative devotional activity.

2 Bible Study (30-45 minutes)

Focus (about 5 minutes)

This brief, introductory section should be an activity or question that shows the relevance of today's study to people's lives. Sometimes, the question or activity will relate to something in the journals, so it's a good idea for people to bring them every week.

Dig In (20-30 minutes)

This is the heart of your study. In this section, the goal of the leader is to move the group through the observation and interpretation process. Study the passage for yourself before you look at our questions and make notes of the questions and ideas you come up with. Then pick from the questions or ideas suggested here. We will sometimes include Inside Insights, notes to help you understand the passage better.

Reflect and Respond (5-10 minutes)

This brief section is very important. It's here that you ask the "so what?" questions of application. "How did this study help me, challenge me, relate to my life, etc.?" "What will I do as a result of this, or how has my perspective changed?" Frequently this will be a chance for people to share something from their journals. Sometimes, too, this will be a time for members to do something expressive to show what they got out of the study.

3 Sharing and Prayer (15-25 minutes)

Here's the time where you allow people to talk about what's going on in their lives and pray for one another. You can leave this totally open-ended, or you can use this time to talk more about your journals. Make sure that you actually spend some time (5-10 minutes at least) in prayer and don't just talk about yourselves till it's time to go home. Use the section at the back of the journals to record prayer requests and praises.

Come now, let us reason together

Theme: Introductory meeting. If you haven't used the Discovery Series before, consider starting with this. It will provide a general introduction to the group, introduce the Discovery Bible study series concept and the journal, and give you the opportunity to make a covenant to explore the Bible's answers to these questions together.

Scripture: Isaiah 1:1-20

1 Getting Started (15-20 minutes)

Icebreaker

Here are a couple mixer ideas. The first one's good for learning names, the second for getting to know each other. (These were both taken from *Incredible Meeting Makers: Mix it Up!* David C. Cook.)

Sentence Sharing

Everyone will need pencil and paper. Have each person write the first initial of each group member's first name down the left hand side of the paper—starting with his or her own name and continuing clockwise around the group. Next, each person has to make a sentence out of all the letters, with each initial being the first letter of each word in the sentence. The sentences must make sense and can't use any of the participants' full names. If people can't make their sentences work, let them rearrange themselves and start over. When they have finished, they should read their acrostic sentences to the rest of the group.

A & Q

Before the session, get some small, square boxes or cube-shaped wooden blocks that can be held in one hand. Tape or glue a label on each side of each box or block. Write the following on the labels (one phrase per label):

a. Yes, but I'll never do that again.

b. Because I was curious.

c. Yes, and I'd do it again if I could.

d. No, and I never would.

e. Because my parents told me to.

f. Yes, but I don't know why.

Explain that people will take turns rolling the cube to see which answer comes up. After rolling the cube, a person must come up with a question that goes with the answer on the cube. For example, a person who rolled the answer, "Because I was curious," might come up with a question like, "Why did I stick my finger in a light socket when I was three?"

Questions must be based on real events in the person's life. Play as many rounds as you have time for.

If you don't have time to tape labels on cubes, simply write the answers on a large sheet of paper, numbered one through six, and have groups roll dice, instead of cubes.

Housekeeping (Today this will take up a larger share of your time.)

Make a break from any goofiness (and allow for the inevitable late-comer) by making necessary announcements after the icebreaker activity and before getting serious. Be brief. Today you'll want to introduce the study series, and nail down the time and length of your meetings.

Introduce the group to the series by saying something like this:

This series is designed to help us explore what the Bible says about who we are as human beings. The Bible's answers are a lot different than society's. The belief that there is a God, and that we were created in His image once gave meaning to human existence. Today this assumption is no longer widely held and people are floundering in a sea of uncertainty. Is this assumption worth revisiting? If you think so, then we're going to spend the next several weeks discussing what the Bible says about our value to God, our uniqueness, and our importance to each other.

Hand out copies of the journals and explain how they can be used.

These journals are not "homework." They are journals. They are meant to stimulate your own self-examination and self-expression. They do, however, introduce the topic that we're going to study the next week so it's best if you set aside some time once or twice a week, at least, to do something in your journal in preparation for our time together.

There is a section each week called "Daily Markings" [flip to that now] where you can keep a daily diary if you want to. The idea is to jot down major events such as an important conversation, a movie you saw, something you read, or something you did that was significant; then write about how you felt about it. The idea is to look back at the end of the week as you've been doing the regular journal and see how God has been at work in your life.

The regular journal section [flip back to that] should be done before the next week's study. It can probably be done in one sitting in about fifteen minutes. But it might be better to spread it out over a couple of days, doing one section or so at a time.

One suggestion is to have the group form prayer partnerships that will meet at least once a week outside of the group time. These partners can share their personal thoughts with each other more deeply than they may in a group setting, and can pray for one another. If you have non-Christians in the group, and we hope you do, this can be especially important. Pair a non-Christian up with a sensitive and mature Christian so that the non-Christian can talk more freely about his or her questions and doubts about Christianity. Encourage the Christians to spend time actually praying together, and not just sharing needs. Nothing bonds two Christians together to produce spiritual growth more than praying together.

Once you have decided when, where, how often, and how long you will meet, decide how you will handle leadership.

Opening

If you have someone who can play an instrument, ask if that person would be willing to lead singing each week. You don't have to sing, of course, but there will be suggestions in this section each week of songs you could sing that go along with the theme. Most of the songs can be found in songbooks available in most Christian bookstores.

Sing a chorus such as "Seek Ye First." Then open your study by asking God to lead you and reveal Himself in whatever way is needed.

There will occasionally be suggestions in this section for creative ways to pray. Invite those who have not committed themselves to Christ, or are unsure, to listen along, but don't put them in a position where they have to lead in prayer.

2 Bible Study (30-45 minutes)

Focus

For this first meeting, just have group members turn to the introduction to the first unit, Do I Matter?, on page 8 of their journals and read it.

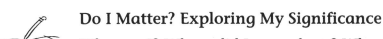

Do I Matter? Exploring My Significance

Who am I? Where did I come from? Why am I here? These are the questions that nag at every thinking human being. Science gives us some answers: Where did you come from? Well, it's like this. Your mother and your father. . . . But that's not really the question, is it? Maybe you need to know if you were wanted by your mother and father. And if the answer is no, then what? Do you matter to anyone? Is there any point to existence at all? If we are simply the highest form that has evolved from the primordial slime, why do we suffer so much asking these pointless questions? Why can't we just be like the fish in the sea or the birds in the air? Somehow we want more.

• **Have any of these questions, or ones like them, bothered you? Are these worthwhile questions to ask?**

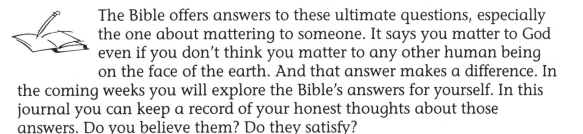

The Bible offers answers to these ultimate questions, especially the one about mattering to someone. It says you matter to God even if you don't think you matter to any other human being on the face of the earth. And that answer makes a difference. In the coming weeks you will explore the Bible's answers for yourself. In this journal you can keep a record of your honest thoughts about those answers. Do you believe them? Do they satisfy?

Point out to your group that sometimes we don't want to hear the answers the Bible gives. The passage you're going to look at right now has some good news and some bad news. It's a message of judgment as well as of mercy. It's primarily a message about God and the claims He makes on those He calls His children.

In the end, it's up to you to decide if you're going to accept the answers the Bible gives or not. So, "Come, now, let us *reason* together" (vs. 18).

Dig In

Explain the "rules of the game" about inductive Bible study from page 8, then move into this quick study in which you will "reason together" about the basic question of God's authority to define our lives. This will not be a thorough inductive study, but will get group members used to the general technique.

Turn in your Bibles to Isaiah 1:1-20. Have someone read the entire text aloud as you all follow along.

Observation Questions:

• Who was this written to and what kind of literature is it? What title would you give this passage?

• Who is said to be speaking from the latter part of verse 2 on? How is this significant?

• From verse 2, what can you tell about the significance of Judah and Jerusalem to God?

• As you read over this passage, what words or phrases stand out to you about what the people are like? To whom does the Lord compare them?

Interpretation:

• Why does the Lord say He "hates" their religious ceremonies? What is it that He wants instead?

• What does God offer the people? What are the terms?

• Do you think this is a fair offer on God's part? Why or why not?

• Why does He say He wants to reason with them? What does this tell you about God?

• If you were to put this chapter to music, what style of music or what instruments would you use? Why?

INSIDE

■ The word "vision" in verse 1 implies that the writer is saying he has a message from God. The author is claiming that he didn't just dream up what he's saying. The prophets of the Old Testament claimed to speak *for* God, and the people accepted their authority as the mouthpieces of the living God. The penalties against false prophets, therefore, were very severe. If just one prophesy proved false, that prophet was to be stoned [Deut. 18:20-22].

Israel was once one nation composed of twelve tribes. After Solomon's death the nation split in two. The northern ten tribes were called Israel, the southern two were called Judah, with Jerusalem the capital. Sometimes when the prophets in this period spoke of Israel it was in reference to the *nation,* the ten northern tribes who broke away from the worship of the Lord. Sometimes it was in reference to the *people* and would have included Judah, which remained somewhat faithful at least in the outward form of their religion. It seems to be the latter here because there is a parallelism between Judah and Jerusalem in the first verse, with Israel and the phrase "my people" in the third verse.

Application:

• Are there things that bother you about this passage? What?

Encourage openness here. In our day when tolerance is often considered the highest virtue, it may be hard for some people to take the concept of God's judgment. That's often the biggest stumbling block that keeps people from coming to Christ. But until a person acknowledges God's right to be God—to call the shots—he or she cannot really come to Christ at all. That's why, in this introductory study we want to hit the issue straight on. Encourage people to be totally honest about their feelings about this kind of a God. Remember, He does not need our defense, He can speak for Himself. A person must accept or reject Him on His own terms.

• Does anyone have a right to judge anyone else? Why or why not? What would give someone a right to judge someone else?

• What difference does belief in God make to a person's self-image?

Wrap up with a summary such as this:

For those who believe in God and accept the Bible as His revealed Word to humanity, there is both good news and bad news. The good news is that we matter to God. He loves us and wants to bless us, as verses 18 and 19 say. But there is always a condition to His blessing. If God is God, then He has a right to lay His conditions on us. They may be for our own good, but we still resist. There are some people who cannot believe in God because they cannot live with the idea of submitting to anyone else's will. If they're right, they haven't lost anything. But if they're wrong, they will suffer the consequences of their rebellion.

What we're going to do in this study is take a look at the biblical foundation for a Christian self-image. Let's reason together. Does it make sense? Does it ring true? The answer is up to you. But remember, whatever you believe, you must be prepared to live with the consequences of your beliefs.

 ## Reflect and Respond

Since you have not used your journals yet, just ask for responses to the study or to the idea of doing this series.

• Are you willing to make the commitment to this study? Are you interested in exploring this topic from a biblical point of view and letting the Scripture speak for itself, even if you don't always like what it says?

• **What anxieties or hopes do you have about how this study might change your life?**

If the group is ready for it, make a covenant to meet together for this study for the next fifteen weeks (or however long it will take to cover what you decide to cover). The terms of this covenant might be something like this: to be faithful in attendance, to keep an open mind toward what the Bible has to say, to be supportive of one another, and honest in sharing from their journals with at least one other person in the group.

Seal the covenant by joining hands in prayer, asking God to bless you.

3 Sharing and Prayer

For the rest of your time, allow people to talk about what's going on in their lives and pray for one another. You can leave this totally open-ended, or you can do something different with this time. Here's one idea.

After everyone has had a chance to share and you have spent some time in prayer, take a Polaroid camera and take a picture of each person in the group. Have each person put his or her name and phone number on the back along with an ongoing prayer request or concern. Collect them; then distribute them as prayer cards. If you're dividing into prayer partners, this is a natural. But even if you're not, this is a good way to get people praying for each other. If you wish, you can ask people to bring the cards back next week and trade them so that everyone will have prayed for everyone else by the time this series is over.

Remind people to do Week One in their journals for next week. Then close in prayer and go eat some goodies!

UNIT One
Do I Matter?
Exploring My Significance

Part of the search for identity is knowing whether we matter to anyone. Not only does our materialist, secular worldview eat away at this hunger for meaning and significance; so does our modern throwaway culture that values only the strong, the beautiful, the "useful," the entertaining.

The Bible's answer is Yes! You Matter. You matter to God even if you don't think you matter to any other human being on the face of the earth. Even if you think you don't matter in this society. The Bible says you matter in this world. And you matter for eternity, and the choices you make in this life have consequences not just for today, but for forever.

This five-week series examines what the Bible says about our significance to God and the sense of purpose, value, hope, and power that can give us in this life. These studies are relevant to Christians as well as those who aren't yet sure what they believe about God and the Bible. A lot of people have some pretty warped ideas about what the Bible teaches about salvation and the Christian life. These studies should set some of those straight and enable people to make a clear decision for Christ or continue to grow in Him.

About the author: These next five studies were written by me, series editor, Anne Dinnan. I've been in, and led a lot of Bible studies, including a few with seekers and skeptics. That, and my natural philosophical bent, makes me acutely sensitive to the questions nonbelievers have about Christianity. My approach is not to pull any punches. This unit lays the foundation of what the Bible says about you. As one who has spent many dark, lonely nights pondering the question of my significance, the answer comes ringing through—I now know, in the depths of my being, that I matter to God. That He not only loves me, He "delights" in me (Ps. 37:23). My prayer is that everyone in your group will find that He delights in you, too.

WEEK 1

Accidentally or on Purpose?

Theme: I have value because I am created in the image of God.

Scripture: Psalm 139

1 Getting Started

Housekeeping

Welcome everyone to the Bible study. If you have new people, make introductions. Then make whatever announcements you need to make at this time. Keep it short.

Icebreaker

Here are two options. In the first you will have your refreshments now instead of later, but you'll use them as your opening activity. If you'd rather not set a precedent of eating during the study, try the other activity.

Homemade or Store-bought?

Bake a batch of homemade chocolate chip cookies. Also buy a popular store-bought brand of the same for a blind taste-test. Ask volunteers to see who can identify the homemade cookies from the store-bought ones. Hint: stay away from the fresh-baked kind that you find at your local mall. Blindfold your volunteers and give them a bite each from a homemade and a storebought cookie.

• **Which cookie is homemade and which is store-bought? Which is better?**

(We sure hope they all say the homemade ones!) Take the blindfolds off and debrief.

• **Why do we generally prefer homemade cookies to store-bought?**

There may be a few exceptions, but most people prefer home-baked goods. Store-bought cookies are mass-produced. They're good, but it's just not the same.

Keep the cookies (and something to wash them down with) at hand for munching during the meeting if you feel comfortable doing so.

I Made It Myself

Bring some object that you have made to your small group to start a time of Show-and-Tell. It could be anything, but should be something you take great pride in, such as a poem you've written, a piece of artwork, a musical composition, an article of clothing, soapbox derby car, model, or something you made as a kid and have kept all these years.

Then go around the room and have people tell about something they once made, that they are still proud of. Affirm each person's contribution as you learn new things about each other. (If you can, call group members and tell them to bring something to group so they can show as well as tell.)

• **Have you ever had anything you made destroyed by someone else or by accident? How did you feel? Why do we feel so strongly about the things we make?**

The Bible says that each of us is not just the product of the union of the egg and sperm of our biological parents, but that we are the personal handiwork of the Creator God. That's an amazing concept.

Opening

Pick a song with the theme of being precious in God's sight, such as "I Was in His Mind" etc.

Ask someone to open in prayer, possibly using something from the prayer they wrote on page 15 of their journals.

2 Bible Study

Focus

Ask people to share something, whether a question or an insight, from the Bible study in their journals this past week. To prompt them you could ask questions like these:

• The Bible is not a science text book, but it's not a book of fairy tales either. What can you say from your study and thoughts this week about the question of science versus the Bible?

You won't have time to get into this too heavily, but there may be people who do have a hard time with this question. Christians take various stances with regard to the theory of evolution. If you have background in this area, you could recommend some literature. But for the purposes of today's discussion it's enough to say that the question of origins is not one that can be approached without faith, whether it's faith in a God who is outside the natural world and created it "by the word of his power," or faith in an unproven and unprovable theory, which cannot be tested by the scientific method.

Whether you believe that we were created by a personal God who knows us and loves us, or you believe that we were simply an accident of the processes of nature, God or no God, makes a tremendous difference. The psalmist, David, definitely believed he had been created by God, and that knowledge was not simply an intellectual conviction or religious creed. That knowledge was deeply personal, as we shall see.

Dig In

Read Psalm 139:1-18 for now. You will read the rest of the psalm later.

Leadership Tip

Since Psalm 139 is poetry, try a creative approach to reading it aloud. First of all, you'll all have to read from the same Bible version. You could choose one person who can read interpretatively. Or, read it responsively a verse at a time. Or, pick two readers to read responsively and have the rest of the group join in as a chorus on verses 6, 10, 14, 17, and 18.

Observation questions:

• **What does the writer say is the scope of God's concern for him?**

If you have access to a writing board or can hang up a large sheet of paper, you might want to jot down their observations in a list like the following:

God's concern extends to:

- **my thoughts**
- **where I go**
- **when I'm asleep or awake**
- **my words**
- **my safety**
- **my development in the womb**
- **my body and my health**
- **how long I will live**

If you think the group is missing something, ask a direct question that will help them see what they've overlooked. For instance, "What do you think the psalmist means in verse 5 about being "hemmed in"?

You might want to have the group divide up into pairs or triplets to discuss the next question; then come together after about five minutes to share your thoughts.

• **If this were the only passage of Scripture you had, what would you think about the psalmist's God?**

• **What does the psalmist think of himself, and how does that relate to his view of God?**

• **The psalmist sees being created by God as a very personal thing. How do you think verses 19-22 fit into this psalm about how great God is that He knows me so well?**

At this point, do continue reading Psalm 139, but backtrack, picking it up from verse 7 and reading to the end.

Have a brief impromptu debate. **True or False: When people stop believing in a personal, creator God, their moral behavior deteriorates.**

After arguments have gone back and forth on this issue, wrap it up by pointing out that, whatever you believe, David believed that. He directly attributed his enemies' wickedness and violence to their hatred of God.

• **Is it OK to hate people? What do you think about verses 21 and 22?**

• **What do you notice about verse 23 and 24? What does this tell you about David?**

INSIDE

■ What stands out most in this psalm is the personal nature of the psalmist's relationship with God. The God revealed here is no impersonal force. There is an intimacy like that of a mother and child.

Knowing that God has created him, the psalmist has a positive view of himself. He marvels at his physical body and how he has grown from the womb. There is also a moral component in his relationship with God with hints of rebellion and guilt in verses 7 and 11. He has apparently tried to hide from God at times, but to no avail.

Verses 19-22 may disturb some. David is upset because unbelievers are blaspheming God's name. He may seem to be intolerant. But because David has such reverence for God who knows everything about him and will never leave him, and because that knowledge acts as a restraint on his own behavior, he cannot understand how anyone can act as if God does not exist.

But instead of pointing his finger at others, David ends this psalm by inviting God to point the finger at him. He invites God to show him his sin and to make him more righteous. Whatever David's feelings are toward those who blaspheme God's name, he leaves it up to God to take any action against them.

Reflect and Respond

Close your study with a couple questions for personal application and reflection.

• **What stands out to you in this psalm?**

• **How do you think David would have answered the question, "Do I Matter?" What would his reasons have been?**

Ask if there was anything anyone wanted to talk about from the journal at this point, or from your study just now. What conclusions would they come to on the question of how our beliefs about God affect our feelings of significance.

You might want to zero in on the prayer section from page 15 of the journal about the voices we hear all around us that contradict what God says about us in the Bible. Allow people to share their thoughts or something they wrote on that.

Get some feedback on how people are doing with the journal. Remind them that they will get much more out of the study if they've thought through some of these things by writing in their journals the week before.

3 Sharing and Prayer

Now have a general time of sharing personal concerns and prayer requests. Make sure to allow at least ten minutes for prayer. You may want to divide up into prayer partners so they can get used to praying together. Prayer partners should meet together (or over the phone) at least once during the coming week to pray for each other. If you know you have nonbelievers there, be sensitive to whether they are ready for something like this. Never force a non-Christian to do something he or she is not comfortable doing (but do stretch the Christians in your group!).

If you want to, close with another song such as: "Search Me, O God."

WEEK 2 Trash or Treasure?

Theme: God's plan of redemption shows my value.

Scripture: Titus 3:3-8; Romans 5:6-8

1 Getting Started

Housekeeping

Welcome people to the group, especially any new members, and make any announcements you need to make.

Icebreaker

The T. P. Game

Pass around a roll of toilet paper and instruct people to tear off as many sheets as they think they'll need. Don't say what they'll need them for, let them assume the obvious. When they've all got as much as they think they'll need, say: **For every sheet you've torn off you need to tell us one thing about yourself.**

Some may have done this before, but don't let them give it away. Whether a person tears off one or two sheets or a whole gob, it will no doubt cause a lot of laughter.

Three Treasures

Ask this familiar mixer question: **If your house were burning down and you only had time to grab three things, what would you grab and why? Or, what three things would you not want to see burned. Why?**

Follow up this question with another one: **Name three belongings that you've had the longest. Why have you kept them so long?**

It should be interesting to discuss whether most people named the same three things or different ones, and why.

Opening

Read Matthew 10:29-31 from the first page of today's Journal. Ask people to meditate quietly on this passage as if Jesus were actually saying it to them. Then open with a prayer of thanks.

2 Bible Study

For only a penny you can buy two sparrows, yet not one sparrow falls to the ground without your Father's consent. As for you, even the hairs of your head have all been counted. So do not be afraid; you are worth much more than many sparrows.

Focus

Ask volunteers to share something from either the Reflection section or the Response section of their journals for this week or read the following true story. It's a pretty good illustration of the concept of redemption. Discuss it as a picture of salvation.

Know the expression "One man's trash is another man's treasure"? One young couple certainly found that to be true. They worked, as a side-line, in the junk business. They'd go out with their van on garbage day and scour the old, rich neighborhoods of their town collecting what other people had thrown away. One day, they found an old, beat-up Oriental rug. It was filthy—full of dog poop, ground-in dirt, and all kinds of stains. It stunk, but they took it, had it professionally cleaned and repaired a bit, and sold the thing for a couple thousand dollars.

The rug's true value came, not from its condition when they found it, but from the quality of its workmanship, the durability of its material, and the experience of its maker. Given the material it was made of, and the skill of the one who made it, it could be restored to close to its original condition. In other words, it could be redeemed. Too bad the people who threw it out did not recognize its true value.

Dig In

Ask someone to read Titus 3:3-8.

• **What are your observations about this passage?**

• **In what ways can people be deceived and enslaved by pleasures and their own passions?**

• **Do you think there's a connection between addiction and violence? Why might there be?**

• **Who takes the initiative in this passage? Why is that important?**

• **Why did God save us? How did He save us?**

Take a look at the words the writer uses to describe what salvation is. Ask the group to define each of them. Here they are, take a crack at it yourself:

- washing
- rebirth
- renewal
- justified

• **Contrast verse three with verse seven. How are we described in this before/after contrast?**

If you used the rug illustration, how is this like that? Talk about the implications of verse three.

• **How does sin affect our self-image? What's the remedy?**

• **Verse eight says that "these things are excellent and profitable for everyone." Why is it profitable to stress these things, and how does this verse say it should affect our lives?**

Now discuss how people answered the question on page 21 of the Journal this week on Romans 5:6-8. Read the verses and discuss people's answers.

Why? (I.e., why did Christ die for us?)

• **How does the cross show God's love for us?**

What does the cross show about our condition? What does it show about our worth?

Why does the Apostle Paul talk about the "offense of the cross" (Galatians 5:11 and I Corinthians 1:23)?

Leadership Tip

This might be an appropriate time to share God's plan of salvation. Follow up the above discussion with the following verses, often called "The Romans Road."

Say something like this: **The Bible puts it pretty clearly. Romans 3:23 says, "For all have sinned and fall short of the glory of God." And in 6:23, it says, "For the wages [the payment or result] of sin is death, but the gift of God is eternal life in Christ Jesus our Lord." We can receive that gift by simple, but profound act of faith. Romans 10:9 says, "That if you confess with your mouth, 'Jesus is Lord,' and believe in your heart that God raised him from the dead, you will be saved."**

Allow people time to wrestle with the implications of confessing Jesus as Lord and believing in their hearts that He has triumphed over death through the resurrection. You could perhaps share what that means to you.

 ## Reflect and Respond

If you shared the Romans Road, continue with a time of sharing. If you didn't, you might instead want to give people a chance to share what they did in the Reaction section of their journals.

 Jesus said, "I have come to seek and to save that which was lost" (Luke 19:10). Read the parable of the Lost Sheep in Luke 15:1-7 and use your creativity to journal your reaction.

• Did you identify with the sheep in this parable? How did you feel about Jesus?

3 Sharing and Prayer

There may be someone who is ready to confess Jesus as Lord right now. Don't let that opportunity pass, but don't push it either. Offer to have someone pray with anyone who is ready or who has more questions. If you're prepared ahead of time for the possibility, someone could just quietly take the person aside, perhaps to another room while the rest of the group is praying. Ask the Holy Spirit for guidance.

In any case, have a time of sharing needs and requests. People can use the pages in their journals to record specific requests and praises. After people have shared their needs, ask two or three volunteers to pray and have one of them close by giving thanks for your time together and for the food you're about to eat.

INSIDE

■ The word "Gospel" means "good news," but it's really a bad news/good news kind of thing. The bad news that the Bible teaches, and that so many people find offensive, is the whole idea of sin and the need for sacrifice. First of all, we don't like to think of ourselves as sinners. Second, the idea of a blood sacrifice seems so barbaric and primitive to our ears. It seems somehow horrible that God's Son should have to die for me. But Hebrews 9:22 says that "without the shedding of blood there is no forgiveness." What the cross shows, and what we have a hard time accepting, is the horror of sin—that God had to take such drastic measures to take care of our problem.

The Gospel must be *bad news* before it can be good news. In I Corinthians 1:23, we find out this is not a modern hang-up. The Jews and Greeks of the ancient world stumbled over this too. Paul called it "the offense of the cross" in Galatians 5:11.

But the fact that Christ was willing to sacrifice His life for us shows how valuable we are to God, even though we're sinners and deserve death. This is the good news, that through Christ's blood shed on the cross our sins are covered and we are forgiven, washed, made clean, and reconciled to God.

Meaningless or Meaningful?

Theme: I can have purpose in life.

Scripture: Ephesians 2:1-10

1 Getting Started

Housekeeping

Welcome and announcements.

Icebreaker

Trivial Pursuit™

Before group, try to get your hands on a game of Trivial Pursuit™ or some other trivia game or quiz. Pull out a stack of cards (two or three times as many as you have group members). Play a round of the game so that each person gets asked all the questions on one card (trade off who reads and who answers, letting someone ask you as well). Keep playing with more cards until all but one person is eliminated by a three-strikes-you're-out rule. Offer a prize of something meaningless such as a piece of bubble gum to the winner. You might want to also offer prizes to any who answered all the questions on any one card correctly.

Ask: **How many of the questions in this game were about things that really mattered, that really made a contribution? What kinds of things would you want to be remembered for? What is it that gives your life meaning?**

Bubble Head

Or, if you prefer, go outside and have a bubble-blowing contest. The person who blows the biggest bubble, or the person whose bubble stays aloft or goes the farthest gets to take the bubbles home. (By the way, if by any chance it happens to be winter and below zero outside, try this anyway. We hear the bubbles freeze as soon as they're blown, and that would be really cool to do too.)

Debrief with some deep philosophical question like: **So, what really is the meaning of life, anyway? Aren't we all like little bubbles floating in a vast universe, only to burst into nothingness? Is God just a great big bubble-blower, spewing us out only to watch us burst at the slightest touch of His finger?**

Opening

If people aren't depressed enough already if you did the bubble contest, try playing the old Kansas song, "Dust in the Wind" if you can find it. Any song that asks the question, "What's the point?" about life would be appropriate. Then sing or read something that affirms that there is meaning to life. Use your imagination.

Pray around a circle, if people feel comfortable, with sentence prayers of thanks to God for what is meaningful in life.

2 Bible Study

Focus

Go around the group and have each person tell how he or she used to answer the question, "What do you want to be when you grow up?"

Do you still have the same dreams or not? How have your plans changed? Why? What discouragements have you faced in the last couple of years about your future?

If people are willing to be that vulnerable, allow volunteers to share what they did on page 27 of their Journals.

Have you ever thought of why you were born who you are and not somebody else? Maybe you wish you had been born into better, easier, happier circumstances. God knows. In your own way, reflect on these questions. Any clue as to what purpose there may be for you being who you are?

Mirror, Mirror, on the wall,

Why am I who I am at all?

Dig In

Read Ephesians 2:1-10. This kind of follows up on what you discussed last time, as it's another explanation of what salvation is and what it does for us.

• **There's a before and an after in this passage, and a lot of contrasts. What does it say about how the people used to live and why?**

• **Who were they following and what was the result of that way of life?**

• **What else do you notice in verses 1-3?**

There's some pretty strong imagery in these verses. It says they were dead, that there was some kind of a spirit at work in them, that they were disobedient, and that they were objects of wrath. Not a very positive picture of life without Christ.

• **Who is the "ruler of the kingdom of the air"?** (See Inside Insights on the next page.)

• **What's the biggest difference between the before and after of these people's lives?** (vs. 4).

• **How were they saved?** (See below for a definition and explanation of grace.)

• **What do you think it means that "God raised us up with Christ and seated us with him in the heavenly realms"? What's Paul getting at here? Does verse 7 help? How?**

This difficult verse refers to a spiritual reality. Someday Christians will be literally raised with Christ and will sit with Him in heaven. But this passage indicates that God is treating us right now as if we were already there.

• **What does verse 10 say about us?**

• **What does this passage say is the purpose for our salvation? Is it just so that we can go to heaven when we die and not have to suffer eternally in hell for our sins?**

• **Is this a new thought for you? How does it make you feel about yourself?**

• **What kinds of "good works" do you think he's talking about? What kind of "good works" do you remember people for? Do they have to be big things? Give an example.**

If you played Trivial Pursuit™ earlier you can probably think of a lot of examples of significant things people have done or discovered that have helped the world (and of course, a lot of bad examples, too).

Reflect and Respond

Explain the meaning of the word *workmanship* from verse 10, then hand out paper or have people use an empty space in their journals, and write down what they think the poem of their lives might look like. Remember, this is from God's perspective, what He thinks of you if you belong to Him (and He wants us all to belong to Him). Assure them not to worry about literary greatness. It doesn't have to rhyme or anything. It could be something as simple as a list of the kind of good works they think God's got planned for them to do. Some people may prefer to doodle than write.

Take several minutes to do this, perhaps with quiet music in the background. Then let volunteers share. Some may prefer to keep theirs private. Honor that.

Close by reading the benediction (the "good word") from Ephesians 3:20, 21. Hold hands in a circle.

Now to him who is able to do immeasurably more than all we ask or imagine, according to his power that is at work within us, to him be glory in the church and in Christ Jesus throughout all generations, for ever and ever! Amen.

INSIDE INSIGHTS

■ The "ruler of the kingdom of the air" is a reference to Satan who was a created being, but not earthbound as we are. He is a *spirit,* and an angel, who out of pride disobeyed God and rebelled against Him. Many scholars think that the lament about the rebellious king of Tyre in Ezekiel 28 is really the story of Satan, and that the king is being compared to Satan. This verse in Ephesians is doing the same thing. There's no neutral ground. You don't have to be a Satanist; if you're not yet a Christian, you are a follower of Satan.

"Grace" is defined as God's undeserved favor. Some use an acronym, God's Riches At Christ's Expense. It is the mercy and help of God in our lives. When we can't help ourselves, He is there.

The word "workmanship" in verse 10 is from a Greek word, *poema.* It's the same word from which we get the English word poem. In other words, we are God's poetry, His work of art, His masterpiece.

3 Sharing and Prayer

Open it up for people to talk about what they got out of tonight's study, and then for a time of general sharing of each other's joys, concerns, and frustrations. Use the pages at the back of the Journal to record both praises and requests. Have a couple people lead out in prayer, or open it up to anyone who wants to. Then encourage people to keep up with their journals for next week and bless the food.

Before you leave, if the mood is still there, say the benediction again before you dismiss.

What's to Look Forward To?

Theme: I can have hope for the future.

Scripture: Philippians 3:12–4:1

1 Getting Started

Housekeeping

Begin thinking of an activity you can do once this unit is over. See next week's Housekeeping section for suggestions.

Icebreaker

Ask one or the other of the questions in the Reflection section on page 35 of the Journals as today's mixer.

List some of the things you most look forward to. What is it that makes each worth waiting for? For example:

My birthday

Christmas

Getting married

 Imagine you are 81 years old looking back on your life. How do you feel?

What is it that has made your life worthwhile?

How do you feel about your impending death? What then?

Opening

Sing something with the theme of questions about the future or trust in God for the future, such as "Precious Lord," or "I Don't Know about Tomorrow . . ." Then ask someone to open in prayer.

2 Bible Study

Focus

Ask volunteers to talk about a time they had a goal that was difficult to stick to. What were the rewards of sticking with it? Why was it hard? Etc.

You could use illustrations from athletics, academics, music, a career, or whatever. The point is that if the goal is worthwhile, it's worth it to stick it out and endure hardship.

Then ask: **Have you ever been in a situation where you had a goal and you stuck with it, but it turned out not to be worth it? How did that feel?**

 ## Dig In

Read today's passage together, Philippians 3:12–4:1.

Observations on the passage:

• **What is it the writer has not already obtained?** (What is the context of this passage?)

• **What is his ultimate goal? What do you notice about this goal?**

• **What is the "therefore" there for in 4:1?** (In other words, look back at the previous verses to see why he said they should stand firm in the Lord.)

• **What would you title this passage?** (And don't just use the title the editor used in your Bible, since those are not inspired.)

Interpretation:

• **How is the Christian life different from other ways of life? What makes it different?**

• **What kind of imagery does the writer use in this passage? How do these images help you understand what the Christian life is all about?**

There are usually two ways to become a citizen of a country. The usual way is to simply be born there. The other most common way is to become a legal resident, study the history and laws of the country and take an oath of allegiance. Quite often, when people become citizens of one country, they must give up their citizenship in their country of origin.

• **In which way does a person become a citizen of heaven? What implications does becoming a citizen of heaven have in terms of other allegiances?**

• **The writer talks about some people living as enemies of the cross of Christ. What do you think that means?**

Application:

• **What privileges and responsibilities does citizenship give you in this country? What are the privileges and responsibilities of citizenship in heaven?**

- What are the implications of this passage for your life?
- How are you like Paul in this passage or not like him? Why?

 # Reflect and Respond

In conclusion, have someone read the following story to the group:

Finish the Race

The Barcelona Olympics of 1992 provide one of track and field's most incredible moments.

Britain's Derek Redmond had dreamed all his life of winning a gold medal in the 400-meter race, and his dream was in sight as the gun sounded in the semifinals at Barcelona. He was running the race of his life and could see the finish line as he rounded the turn into the backstretch. Suddenly he felt a sharp pain go up the back of his leg. He fell face first onto the track with a torn right hamstring.

Sports Illustrated recorded the dramatic event:

> As the medical attendants were approaching, Redmond fought to his feet. "It was animal instinct," he would say later. He set out hopping, in a crazed attempt to finish the race. When he reached the stretch, a large man in a T-shirt came out of the stands, hurled aside a security guard and ran to Redmond, embracing him. It was Jim Redmond, Derek's father. "You don't have to do this," he told his weeping son. "Yes, I do," said Derek. "Well, then," said Jim, "we're going to finish this together."
>
> And they did. Fighting off security men, the son's head sometimes buried in his father's shoulder, they stayed in Derek's lane all the way to the end, as the crowd gaped, then rose and howled and wept.
>
> Derek didn't walk away with the gold medal, but he walked away with an incredible memory of a father who, when he saw his son in pain, left his seat in the stands to help him finish the race.

Reprinted from *Hot Illustrations for Youth Talks* by Wayne Rice, © 1994 by Youth Specialties, Inc., 1224 Greenfield Dr., El Cajon, CA 92021. Used by permission.

Close with a time of silent prayer reflecting on the character of God and the fact that, like that father, He runs the race with us, holding us up and giving us the strength we need to finish the course. Then move into your sharing and prayer time.

3 Sharing and Prayer

In addition to taking prayer requests and talking about the events of people's weeks, ask people to share insights and general comments about their Journals this week. Be ready to respond to questions or special needs for prayer.

Then pray for one another. If you have prayer partners, you might want to have them pray aloud before the group for their partner, or pray for the persons on their right or left. Anyway, be sure that everyone in the group is prayed for.

For next week:

Tell people to be thinking of ideas to suggest for an outing when you finish this unit and before you start the next.

Also, if you want to, tell people to bring baby pictures of themselves for an activity next week.

WEEK 5 That Extra Dimension

Theme: I can live a different kind of life.

Scripture: Romans 6:1-23

1 Getting Started

Housekeeping

This is the last week of this unit on exploring our significance. If you continue with the study into the next units you will be changing the focus to exploring your uniqueness, the contributions each individual has to make to the world. It's a good idea this week to look back over the study to see what you've learned and how you've grown. This is also a good time to plan some kind of an event together apart from the study. You may want to skip a week and use your time together for something entirely different, or plan another time to get together.

Do something out of the ordinary. When's the last time anyone went to an art museum? Or, how about a service project like volunteering at your local soup kitchen or homeless shelter? Put your heads together and come up with something that makes sense for you.

Whatever you do, talk about it afterwards in terms of every human being's significance and value to God. How did this study help you see people differently? What did you see or do that was of ultimate value?

Icebreaker

Baby, Just Look at You Now!

If enough people remembered to bring their baby pictures, see who can identify who in a baby picture contest. Have them write their names on the back of the pictures, and without showing them to anyone else, give them to you. You shuffle them and lay them out on a piece of white cardboard or on the floor and have people guess who is who. Keep track of the guesses and award prizes for the person who made the most correct guesses, and the person who was guessed correctly most often.

A twist on this activity, if people did not bring baby pictures, is to have them draw a picture of themselves as very young children and then have people guess who is who.

My, How I've Changed

Just have an open-ended discussion on the question: **How have you changed the most in the last three to five years? Why?**

Opening

A great song to sing this week would the classic hymn, "Amazing Grace." If you don't sing it, try reading it aloud and discussing the words.

2 Bible Study

Focus

Ask people how they responded to the questions in the Reflection section of their journals.

Fruit Picking

Check out what's growing on the tree of your life. For instance, has love ripened in you or are you still pretty green with things like jealousy or selfishness? Is joy blossoming in your heart? What about goodness? Self-control? Etc. Describe the fruit growing in your life.

What quality of the Holy Spirit from Galatians 5:22 do you most need in your life right now?

Dig In

Say something like: **One question almost every Christian asks sooner or later is, "How do I *do* this? I know that as a Christian my life is supposed be a certain way, but how can live up to that level of goodness? How does one live the Christian life?"**

The passage for today answers that question, and it is one of the most important lessons you can learn about what it means to be a Christian. Break the reading up into sections and give people time to read it over again to themselves before you ask questions. This is a difficult passage to grasp.

First, read Romans 6:1-4.

• **Why would anyone suggest that we could go on sinning? What have we learned already about grace?**

(That it's grace that saves us, not our good works. So why not keep sinning if we know we'll still be forgiven?)

INSIDE INSIGHTS

■ In verses 3, 4 Paul discusses baptism. Churches differ in their practice and understanding of baptism today— whether it should be by immersion or sprinkling; whether it's only for believing converts or for infants as well. In either case, baptism is understood by many as the initiation rite for membership in the church. Baptism obviously symbolizes cleansing, but more than that, it symbolizes the believer's identification with Christ in His death, burial, and resurrection. Just as Jesus identified with sinners in His baptism (Matt. 3:13-17; Luke 3:21), so we identify with Christ in our baptism. Paul here indicates that this baptism is more than merely symbolic. (Though that does not mean he's saying that the act of baptism is what saves a person.) But the act of identifying with Christ in baptism means that we recognize our own death to sin and resurrection to new life in Christ.

• **What does Paul say about this reasoning? What does he mean by saying that "we died to sin"?**

Now read verses 5-14, having a different reader read each paragraph (5-7, 8-10, 11-14).

• **What's the writer talking about here? In what sense could a person die with Christ?**

• **Have you ever thought of the crucifixion this way? How is this different from ways you used to think of Christ's death on the cross?**

Some people may have thought of the cross only in terms of Jesus taking the punishment for our sins so that we can go to heaven when we die. But this passage is talking about its having value for this life, and that somehow when Jesus died, we died too. Get people to talk about how this can be.

• **How does Christ's death and resurrection benefit us in terms of our struggle with sin? Why?**

• **What does Paul say (verse 11) as the secret for having victory over sin in our lives?**

• **What is God's part in all of this and what is our part?**

Leadership Tip

You might want to create a chart at this point with two columns: God's Part/Our Part.

Your chart may look something like this:

God's Part	Our Part
Jesus died for us	We identify with Him in His death
Jesus rose from the dead	We count ourselves as alive to God
Our sins died with Christ	We count ourselves dead to sin
Jesus triumphed over sin in His resurrection	We do not offer the parts of our bodies to sin anymore
We have been brought from death to life by Christ	We offer ourselves to God as instruments of righteousness
God gives the power	We believe He's done it and we act upon that belief

• How does this section say that we can live victoriously over sin? Do you think it's really possible to live without sinning?

You may get quite a discussion going here. From these verses alone, it would seem that it is at least theoretically possible to live without sinning, and in fact, that's the ideal that's held up. You might point out that the very next chapter in Romans apparently describes in all too familiar detail the Christian's continual battle with the sin nature. First John 1:8, 9 says "If we claim to be without sin, we deceive ourselves and the truth is not in us. If we confess our sins, he is faithful and just and will forgive us our sins and purify us from all unrighteousness."

Now read the next section, verses 15-23, to get more of Paul's explanation of how to live victoriously over sin.

• In the previous sections, Paul used the metaphor of death and new life. What metaphors or illustrations does he use here? What does this imply?

• What does he say about the Roman Christians (note at least three things)? **How is this encouraging to you?**

• Answer verse 21 for Paul. Give examples of the kinds of things Paul might be talking about. If these things have such horrible consequences, why do we still do them? What does the passage say?

 ## Reflect and Respond

Ask if there's anyone who can relate to this passage. Has anyone experienced being set free from something that had
once enslaved him or her?

• **What has this study shown you about your significance to God?**

• **What hope does this chapter offer to you?**

Have people share insights from their Journals. Give people time to affirm
or question what the Bible teaches about human value and each individual's significance to God.

3 Sharing and Prayer

Give people more time to share their thoughts or creations from page 46 of
their journals. Also, go over some of the answers to prayer you've seen in
your time together and give people a chance to give their reactions to the
study, the Journal, prayer partners, or anything else you've done. Be open
to criticism, but in general this should be a positive time.

• **Did this study really answer the questions you had?**

• **What questions do you still have?**

• **How have you changed as a result of this time?**

• **What could we do as a group to improve the atmosphere of this
group?**

After praying for specific requests of the group, close with a prayer time following the pattern on page 47 of the journal. If you want, you could just go
around a circle having people read what they wrote one section at a time.
(Of course, if someone didn't do that part, they could just say something on
the spot or else pass.)

Sing "Amazing Grace" one more time, or a favorite chorus.

UNIT Two

One of a Kind

Exploring My Uniqueness

Part of knowing who we are and having a sense of value has to do with our sense of competence to face the world. All people need the affirmation that they are valued for who they are and that they have a contribution to make in this world. Face it, we all have faults and inadequacies. But part of being made in the image of God is the beauty that remains (fallen though we are) in the variety of our personalities. Being human can be awfully fun when we live in the knowlege that God created us as we are for His pleasure as well as for His service.

About the authors: *This series was written by a husband and wife team. Alyce T. and David Reimer are well acquainted with the struggles of this aspect of identity. David is a professional violinist, trying to make it in his career. He's written his own Bible studies for InterVarsity groups for years, but this is the first time he's written anything for publication, and he confesses finding a new joy in doing so. He wrote weeks seven, eight, and nine. Alyce T., who wrote weeks six and ten, is a staff worker and Evangelism Specialist with InterVarsity Christian Fellowship. She grew up in inner-city Boston and became a Christian in her early twenties. Alyce reports coming alive to the things of the mind as well as the Spirit when she was converted and has her degree in Biblical and Theological Studies from Gordon College in Wenham, Mass. She loves writing poetry, reading children's literature, bird-watching, and a thousand other things.*

WEEK 6: You Are Just Like . . . You!

Theme: God's design is evident in the uniqueness of my personality.

Scripture: Judges 4:1-16; 5:1-3, 7-9, 12 (Deborah); Judges 6:1-17, 25-27 (Gideon); Judges 14 (Samson)

1 Getting Started

Icebreaker

Try one of these activity ideas:

Unique Marks!

Gather two objects for every person in your group. These objects should differ from each other in type, color, size, etc. Prior to the meeting have the objects artistically displayed around the room. Have each person choose an object and share one aspect of it that appealed to him or her. After the Bible study they will share again using the object. If possible, allow each person to keep his or her chosen object.

What's in a Name?

Make sure you have access to a good name book. Ask what people's names mean. Ask if anyone knows why their parents named them what they did, or if there are unique stories behind their names, nicknames, etc. If time allows, note in the Scripture that the changing of names occurs quite a bit. Check these passages out: Gen. 17:5, 15; Gen. 32:28; II Samuel 12:25; John 1:42; Acts 4:36, 13:9; and Proverbs 22:1.

Housekeeping

Welcome people and introduce newcomers. It's announcement time again. Be creative with this time or choose someone else to do the announcements. Perhaps in skit form. Be brief.

Opening

Read, or have an expressive reader read the poem on page 52 of your journal. Then open with a quick prayer thanking God for the uniqueness of our personalities.

2 Bible Study

Focus

Use the Reflection section on page 53 of your journals to begin this study.

Pick several ice-cream flavors that best describe your personality. Explain why.

• **What did you say/write in response to these two questions?**

Our study today focuses on three very distinct individuals from the Book of Judges.

Dig In

Read, or summarize the brief explanation of the Book of Judges below. You will be looking at three very different characters to contrast their personalities and see how God used them to lead Israel despite their weaknesses.

Write "Personality Marks of" across the top of a large sheet of paper; then make three column headings, one each for Deborah, Gideon, and Samson. It's best if you can use markers and tape the paper to a wall or something. Half a sheet of poster board might be better if you don't have wall space.

Deborah

Deborah's story is found in Judges chapters 4 and 5. Read these verses to get the gist of the story: 4:1-16. Then have a guy and a gal read parts of Deborah and Barak's song in 5:1-3, 7-9, 12 to get more insight into Deborah's personality.

• **From what you know of Israel's history or those days in general, would it have been common to have had a woman lead a nation? What does that say about her?**

• **Who is the stronger character in this story? What does it say about Barak that he wanted Deborah to go with him? What does it say about Deborah that he wanted her to go with him?**

• **What does the song reveal about Deborah, about what matters to her and what she thinks of herself?**

• **Do you know anyone like Deborah?**

• **What words would you use to describe Deborah's personality?**

Write responses in the Deborah column on your Personality Markers chart.

Gideon

Gideon was the next to judge Israel. Some people might be very familiar with his story about the fleece. We're not going to look at that part (although you may if you have time). We'll just concentrate on the earlier part when God first called him, because his personality comes out so clearly in these verses. Have someone read Judges 6:1-17.

• **What do you notice about Gideon right away in this story?**

INSIDE

■ The Book of Judges is one of the most colorful books in the Bible—full of blood, guts, and scandal of every imaginable kind. It almost makes our own day seem tame by comparison. The theme is summed up in this phrase repeated throughout the book: after so-and-so died, "the people did evil in the eyes of the Lord," so the Lord sold them into the hands of their enemies. The last verse of the book says, "In those days Israel had no king; *everyone did as he saw fit.*"

Consequently, even some of the good guys were rather checkered characters. But God used them anyway when they responded to Him in faith and obedience. After a period of decline when the people began to suffer at the hands of their enemies, they would remember God and cry out to Him for deliverance. Time and time again, God would raise up a judge to deliver Israel from her enemies and rule over the nation in peace for a period of time till they once again forgot God and did evil in His eyes.

Begin to write these on your chart. Don't worry if you get disagreement on these responses. Some people may read Gideon one way, some another. That just goes to show that people are complex.

• **What does God say about Gideon?** (vs. 14)

• **What does Gideon say about himself, and what is God's response?**

• **What strikes you about Gideon's dialogue with God?**

• **How would you describe his personality from this?**

Record more responses. Then read verses 25-27 and record more impressions of Gideon's personality from this part of the story.

• **Do you know anyone like Gideon?**

• **Why do you think God used him?**

This is a question for speculation. You would have to study the rest of the story as a whole to get a better picture, but some people may have some good insights. (If you have time, you might want to peek at the end of the story and read 8:22-28.)

Samson

Of all the characters in the Book of Judges, Samson may be the most colorful and intriguing. The story of Samson and Delilah is pretty familiar, but we're going to look at an earlier part to catch a glimpse of Samson's personality. Read all of chapter 14 and list people's observations about his personality on your Personality Marks chart. Use questions like these to get your list.

• **What words would you use to describe Samson?**

• **Do you think you'd like him? Why or why not?**

• **Describe a situation in which you'd like to be around Samson, and one when you wouldn't. Why?**

• **How was Samson as a son? With women? With his friends? With his enemies?**

Again, if you have time, you could read something from the end of the story to expand on the previous question and ask how Samson was with God. Read Judges 16:23-31.

• **Why do you think God used a person like Samson? How could his life have turned out differently?**

Summary

• **Are there any personality traits that you share with Deborah, Gideon, or Samson?**

• **Would you want any of them as a friend? Why?**

• **What interested you most about these three characters and why God used them? What can you learn from this?**

There's a difference between personality and character. Personality is something inborn, it more or less is a package deal. You can't change your basic personality. But each personality characteristic can be used either for God or for self. Character refers to the moral quality within our personalities which we can develop either for good or for evil. Next week we will talk more about this when we talk about strengths and weaknesses.

• **Of the three judges we just studied, which one do you think had the most strength of character? Why?**

Reflect and Respond

Now hand out some scrap paper and have everyone create his or her own Personality Marks list. Give people a few

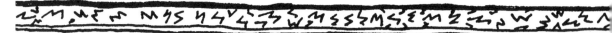

minutes to think about themselves and write down words to describe their personality characteristics. Ask volunteers to share some of their markings.

• **Do you know and can you share your own personality marks?**

• **What about your marks excites you?**

• **What about your marks do you find hard to accept?**

• **Who or what do we attribute our personalities to?**

Now challenge the group with the question: **If God could use a Deborah, a Gideon, or a Samson, how do you think God could use someone with your personality for His purposes?**

• **What can you say thank-you to God for about your personality?**

(If you used the "Unique Marks!" icebreaker, now is the time to share another reason for choosing it. If people take these objects, the assignment is as follows: At least once a week look at the object as a reminder that God can and does use ordinary things for His purposes. Write in your journal about one aspect of your God-designed personality. Write as well how you can use your unique personality to enrich others in their lives.)

(If you chose the "What's in a Name?" activity, ask how do we live up to our names? Think of a name other than your own that perfectly suits your personality.)

3 Sharing and Prayer

Often people don't know how to celebrate the gifts God has given them. During this time, let the prayer be first focused on affirming the personality traits in each other. Next, let there be applause and thanksgiving prayers to God for all our personalities. Finally, in silence, listen for God's promptings about how He wants to use all of your personalities in His service.

WEEK 7

Living with Strengths and Weaknesses

Theme: I have value in spite of my imperfections.

Scripture: Genesis 12—13:4

1 Getting Started

Housekeeping

Welcome everyone to the Bible study. If you have new people, make introductions. Then make announcements.

Icebreaker

Three Things

Have each person think of two little-known facts about him or her and make up a third. As each shares, the group attempts to guess which thing is not true. If you wish to score the game and bring a gag gift for the "winner," have the group write down their guesses for each person and compare the number of correct guesses at the end.

Opening

If you know it, sing the chorus "Father Abraham" and then ask someone to open in prayer.

2 Bible Study

Focus

Ask people to share their impressions of who Abraham was. Some may have biblical answers such as Father of the Jews, the Father of faith, Father of the Arab race (through Ishmael), the man who almost sacrificed his son, etc. Others may have erroneous answers or no answer at all. For the function of this introduction, no corrections need be made of what is shared. (N.T. references to Abraham: John 8:31-58, Romans 4, Hebrews 11:1-3, 8-19, James 2:18-24.)

Dig In

Divide your study into the following sections, Who God Is, God's Grace and Abram's Strength, Abram's Other Side, and finally, Who Is Abram Really?

Who God Is

Read Genesis 12:1-8.

• **What God says tells us a lot about Him. Who is God?**

(Make sure that of all the points that are brought out, this is understood: God is a person, not an impersonal force—a who, not a what.)

• **What are God's promises to Abram?**

• **What does He mean by "all peoples"?**

• **What kind of power does God give to Abram?**

• **What would it be like if verse 3 were promised to you today?**

• **What is God's purpose in this speech?**

• If God can make these promises and fulfill them, what does that say about Him?

God's Grace and Abram's Strength

Now turn your attention to Abram from this same section of the text.

• **Who is Abram?**

• **What has Abram done to earn this incredible promise?**

• **Could anyone really deserve such a blessing?**

• **What risks does Abram face in receiving and obeying this decree?**

• **What action does he take in response to God?**

• **What strengths does Abram display in this passage?**

Abram's Other side

Now read Genesis 12:9—13:4.

• **Does Abram's decision reflect moral failure? If so, how does he fail and what are the costs of his failure?**

• **What influenced his poor choice?**

• **How might he have acted differently?**

• **What weaknesses are apparent in this passage?**

Who Is Abram Really?

Point out that verse 13:4 is a repetition of 12:8.

• **As a frame around the incident in Egypt, what does this say about Abram's relationship with God?**

• **Has God given up on him or retracted His blessing?**

• **What is the fuller picture that you have of Abram now?**

Make a list Abram's strengths and weaknesses.

Reflect and Respond

• **What have you learned about God and about human beings from this passage?**

• **What can you emulate from Abram's life?**

• Does God require perfection to accomplish His purposes? What does He require?

Read the list, "Qualities of Character" on page 64, or copy it and give everyone a copy. As you read it, have people rate whether they are strong or weak in each quality. Encourage people to share:

• What are your strengths and weaknesses?

• How might God be desiring to work through both your strengths and weaknesses?

3 Sharing and Prayer

Abram "built an altar" and "called on the name of the Lord." Respond to Abram's worship by using the A.C.T.S. acronym for prayer. Here's a suggested format with hymns, choruses, and other readings if you want to make this more of a worship time.

A—Adoration

Using sentence prayers, praise the Lord for the attributes and actions observed in the passage. You may want to incorporate hymns, choruses or other Scripture passages in declaring who God is.

(Hymns: "Great God of Wonders"; "Praise to the Lord, the Almighty"; "The God of Abraham Praise"; "Great Is Thy Faithfulness." Choruses: "Praise Him"; "Awesome God"; "We Exalt Thee"; "Father I Adore You"; "Glorify Thy Name"; "Great is the Lord"; "O, Come Let Us Adore Him.")

(Scripture: Psalms 8, 19, 95, 98; Isaiah 40:21-31; Colossians 1:15-20; Philippians 2:5-11; Hebrews 1; Revelation 4.)

C—Confession

Abram built an altar—a place of sacrifice. Come to God acknowledging that your strengths and weaknesses both pale in comparison to Him. Allow a time of quiet for people to bring their personal failures to God. You may want to use the confession on the following page.

T—Thanksgiving

Thank God for strengths that He has given and the opportunities to use them.

S—Supplication

Commit strengths and weaknesses to God and ask Him to work through them in as concrete and specific ways as possible. Other prayer requests may be included here as well. End with the hymn "I Am the Lord's."

Suggested group activity before the next meeting:

Watch the classic movie, *It's a Wonderful Life* together. (Black-and-white version recommended.)

---

*L*ord,

We confess that we have sinned against You in thought, word, and deed, by what we have done, and by what we should have done, but didn't.

We have not loved You with our whole heart and we have not loved our neighbors as ourselves.

We are truly sorry and we humbly repent.

For the sake of Your Son Jesus Christ, have mercy on us and forgive us;

that we may delight in Your will, and follow You all of our days, to the glory of your Name. Amen.

—adapted from *The Book of Common Prayer*

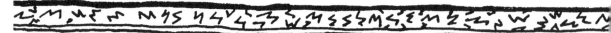

Qualities of Character

love—being committed to someone, to sacrifice for him or her, to give the benefit of the doubt, to hope for that one's best, to care

joy—having an exuberant disposition that comes from knowing that God is emphatically for us

peace—being content with who you are and who God is

patience—being able to wait for God's timing, especially when your own timetable is not being met

benevolence—being kind, merciful, and generous to others

faithfulness—being responsible for your behavior and reliable to follow through on what you have committed to do

courteousness—being gentle in demeanor and respectful to your fellow human beings

self-control—having the ability to confront sinful impulses and prevent them from becoming sinful actions; being disciplined

honesty—being truthful with yourself and about yourself

wisdom—having the ability to receive advice, gather information, and make morally appropriate decisions

humility—having an appropriate view of who you are in relation to God and to others, which makes it possible to learn

integrity—being fair and honorable in all of your affairs

resilience—being persistent in the face of trial, able to keep trying time and time again

goodness—being able to know and act on what is right and appropriate, being helpful toward others

excellence—being concerned about the quality of what you do and striving to live accordingly

industrious—having the ability to see an opportunity, make a plan, and work hard to the finish

encouragement—being one to affirm another's worth by verbal and non-verbal means

humorous—being able to bring playfulness and lightheartedness into your everyday life in ways that are appropriate

WEEK 8 Puzzling Over Your Gifts?

Theme: I can make a contribution in this world because God has given me gifts and talents.

Scripture: Character study of Barnabas from the Book of Acts

1 Getting Started

Housekeeping

Welcome everyone to the Bible study. If you have new people, make introductions. Then make whatever announcements you need to at this time. Open in prayer.

Icebreaker

Puzzle exercise

Preparation—(1) Find a puzzle of 150-250 pieces with distinct sections of comparable size, corresponding to the number of people you have in your group. For example, you might find a puzzle with three dogs, a

mailman, a mailbox, and a border, each requiring about 20-30 pieces.
(2) Assemble the puzzle yourself and then break it apart into sections.
(3) Disassemble each section and put the pieces for each in a separate bag.
(4) Remove one piece from each bag and keep it for use in the meeting.

Execution—give a bag to each member of the group to assemble by themselves. When each has finished his or her section, have the group assemble the sections into the complete puzzle. Keep the suspense of the missing pieces until later, allowing members to discuss what happened.

2 Bible Study

Focus

Have people share some puzzle pieces from their own lives.

• **What are the different environments that you find yourself in through the course of a week?**

• **Who do you interact with there?**

Dig In

This Bible study is also like a puzzle. You will read several short passages from the Book of Acts to form a picture of the kind of person Barnabas was. You will also explore the complexity of gifts listed in Scripture and reflect upon your own life and the value of the contribution you can make to the good of those around you.

Ask volunteers to read the following passages and share first impressions of Barnabas as seen from these passages:

Acts 4:32-37

Acts 9:22-28

Acts 13:1-5

Acts 14:8-18

Acts 15:1-13

Acts 15:36-39

Now have volunteers read I Corinthians 12:7-11, 27-31 and Ephesians 4:11-13. On a large sheet of paper or poster board, make a list of all the gifts mentioned; then discuss each one (see the chart on the following page). Try to come up with a definition or general description for how each gift might work in the church.

• **Why is each one important?**

• **Do you know anybody with any of these gifts? Describe.**

When they are finished, ask them to discuss what gifts Barnabas had and which he did not. Review the passages you looked up about him, as necessary.

• **If you are a Christian, you are gifted as well. Which gift or gifts, do you think you may have for service to the body of Christ?**

Have them write these on scraps of paper.

In the Classic movie *It's a Wonderful Life,* George Bailey reaches a crisis in his life. He has led an ordinary life interspersed with noble and heroic episodes, but is haunted by events that thwarted his life's ambitions. As events accelerate which drive him to the brink of despair,

INSIDE INSIGHTS

■ Spiritual gifts are abilities given to every believer by God through the power of the indwelling Holy Spirit. They are not merely human talents or abilities. Their purpose is for service to the rest of the body of Christ so that all may grow more like Christ. There are several passages that contain lists of spiritual gifts. Romans 12:3-8 is one. First Corinthians chapter 12 is the most complete. Verses 7-11 lists gifts in terms of their use in the church without any ranking. Verses 27-31 may give a ranking order of the gifts in terms of leadership. First Corinthians 14 gives instructions for how the gifts are to be used in a worship service or when the congregation meets. A lot of time is given to dealing with the controversial gift of tongues. (Apparently, it was something of a controversy even then. Don't get sidetracked on this issue.)

Another important passage is Ephesians 4:11-13, which lists leadership gifts, but says these are to be used to prepare others to do their part so that the whole body may be built up. First Peter 4:7-11 also seems to refer to such things as hospitality, speaking (probably in the sense of preaching), and service as gifts.

Romans 12: 3-8:	I Corinthians 12:7-11:	I Corinthians 12:27-31:	Ephesians 4:11-13:	I Peter 4:7-11:
Prophesying	Wisdom	Apostles	Apostles	Hospitality
Service	Knowledge	Prophets	Prophets	Preaching
Teaching	Faith	Teachers	Evangelists	Service
Encouraging	Healing	Then miracles, healing, helps, administration, tongues (languages).	Pastors and Teachers	
Giving	Miraculous powers			
Leadership (governing)	Prophecy			
Mercy	Distinguishing between spirits			
	Speaking in tongues (languages)			
	Interpreting tongues (languages)			

George calls on God for help. His answer comes in the form of a guardian angel who allows him to see what his community would look like if he had never been born. What follows is a litany of tragic scenes that had been averted due to George's presence. As his angel says, "Strange, isn't it? Each man's life touches so many other lives. When he isn't around, he leaves an awful hole, doesn't he?"

God is not limited to one way or one person to accomplish His purposes, but consider and discuss the hole that would have been left if Barnabas had not been there in these passages.

• **How many lives did he touch directly and indirectly?**

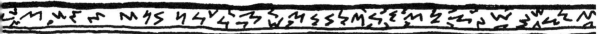

 # Reflect and Respond

Put each member in the spotlight and do the following:

Step One:

• Ask them to share what they wrote in their journals on page 69.

 What do you enjoy doing? What do you think you do well? Make a list.

Do you think others believe you have something to offer? What have you heard people say about your talents? If you're not sure, ask a friend.

• **After today's study, do you have any idea what your spiritual gifts are if you are a Christian?**

Christians can share what they put on their scrap of paper. Allow anyone who does not feel comfortable with this question to simply answer "no," or "I'm not sure," and go on to step two.

Step Two:

• Ask the group to affirm the individual in his or her natural abilities as well as spiritual gifts. There may also be a need, based on how much trust is built in the group, to lovingly challenge the individual about a questionable self assessment. Most people tend to sell themselves short. Use this to offer honest encouragement.

• Ask everyone to consider the hole that would be left by the absence of this individual.

Step Three:

• Give the person a missing puzzle piece and have him/her put it in place on the puzzle.

• Have two people pray for the person, that his or her gifts and abilities may be more evident, and that he or she would receive guidance from the Lord in becoming the person God wants him/her to be. Then move on to the next person.

Close with a song of commitment such as: "Take My Life and Let It Be."

3 Sharing and Prayer

You may want to share prayer requests not related to the study at this point and pray together for them, or you may want to let the previous song be the end of the meeting.

Suggested group activity before next meeting:

Attend a local sporting event together. It could be a high school, college, or professional event. For those who are not fans of sports, suggest that they think of it as a case study in reaching a goal or overcoming adversity. Attending an event is highly preferable, but watching one on television is another option.

WEEK 9 Scoring with God

Theme: My unique interests, goals, and dreams can be used by God.

Scripture: Nehemiah 1—2:9 [11-20]

1 Getting Started

Icebreaker

As members of the group arrive, have a video (or audio) tape running with a game such as baseball, hockey, soccer, basketball, football, etc. When the last person arrives and everyone is settled in, turn off the tape and raise these questions:

• **What involvement have you had with sports either as a participant or a spectator?**

• **What does it take to reach a goal in (team) sports?**

• **What is the coach's part?**

• **How important is it that team members have the same goal and keep it in sight throughout their season?**

Housekeeping

If you are going to have a party next week, your announcements should include the following:

- Pass the hat, or ask people to bring money for food, etc.

- Ask for volunteers to help shop or decorate.

- Tell everyone to be on time for the party. (If you did the activity "Unique Markings" from Week Six, everyone will need to bring back the object they took home for the celebration.)

- You will still need your Bibles and your journals for sharing time.

Opening

Sing or read as a group the hymn "Be Thou My Vision."

2 Bible Study

Focus

Attempt to define "vision" as a group. After some sharing, read the dictionary definition and discuss it in terms of a "vision statement," such as a corporation or organization might have.

- What is a vision or purpose statement?

- If you were to write one for yourself, what would it say?

Dig In

Read Nehemiah chapter 1.

Nehemiah's vision

It would appear that Nehemiah catches his vision in the first four verses. Think about the implications of each verse and discuss the stages of this vision. It may help to list them on a chalkboard or poster board.

Possible stages:

1. Awareness of issues and events (vss. 1, 2)

2. Hearing messages of need (vs. 3)

3. Identifying with the need (vs. 4)

4. Bringing the whole situation before God in prayer (vss. 5-11)

Nehemiah's First Action

Reread Nehemiah 1:5-11.

• **What is Nehemiah's first action step?**

• **How might this action prayer differ from those in verse 4?**

• **Analyze and discuss the elements of Nehemiah's prayer. Why does he say what he says?**

The Rest of Nehemiah's Plan

Now read what Nehemiah did next in 2:1-10.

• **What requests did Nehemiah have mapped out before going to the king?**

• **What dangers did he face in going to the king?**

• **What do you think of his method of reaching the king? Was it intentional?**

• **How might Nehemiah's character and quality of service have aided his getting a hearing?**

• **What does Nehemiah's conversation with the King say about him?**

Often in an athletic event (or any other goal-oriented activity), a team or player loses momentum and vision after overcoming a major obstacle, causing defeat.

• **What foreshadowing do you see of such a situation for Nehemiah? What kind of obstacles might he face?** (For answers, you will have to read the rest of the book!)

Read Nehemiah 6:15.

Reflect and Respond

• Has God given you a vision at this point in your life, or do you see ways that He is preparing you to receive a vision?

• In light of Nehemiah's example, how will you respond to God's preparation and call?

• How can you keep the vision alive through adversity and success?

• Do you have difficulty acting decisively due to fear and other emotions? How so? What can you learn from Nehemiah on this?

• How encouraging is God's extravagant answer to Nehemiah's prayer and action?

• In what way will your vision be different this week due to studying this passage?

3 Sharing and Prayer

Read Isaiah 6:1-8.

Pray together for God to prepare you to receive the vision, for Him to send the vision, and for each person the courage to act on the vision He gives. Close by singing a chorus or hymn such as "Open My Eyes, Lord," or "May the Mind of Christ My Savior."

WEEK 10

Jesus the Party Maker

Theme: I can have meaning and purpose in life now and forever because of Jesus' death and resurrection on my behalf.

Scripture: Luke 24

1 Getting Started

Housekeeping

Be brief here. One thing for sure is to say we will meet at our regular time next week. It is very important to be well prepared for the flow of the party. Here are some ideas for preparation ahead of time.

Food

Chocolate fondue is easy and can be a lot of fun. Oranges, grapes, pineapple, bananas, strawberries, and apples are fruits that go well with chocolate. You can also dip marshmallows, vanilla wafers, or chunks of pound cake. Get a pound of your favorite plain (no nuts) chocolate bars, or a bag of good quality milk chocolate chips.

A fondue pot is great, but you don't need one. You can use either a double boiler or two pots of similar size. Fill the bottom pot halfway with water. Put the chocolate in the other pot and set it on top of the other one. Keep your heat low to medium and bring the water to a slow, rolling boil. It should take about fifteen to twenty minutes.

Serve it right away. If your chocolate starts getting hard again, stick it back on the stove to reheat for about five minutes.

Icebreaker

It's Party Time

Have music going in the background as people arrive. You might want to have instrumental music on very low throughout the evening, except during your discussion. As part of the party, have people get involved in cutting up the fruit. Make sure the chocolate fondue is heating at the very start of the party. Ask for a volunteer to serve the beverages and another to hang up coats. The idea is for all of you to be putting on the party while enjoying it. Start eating the dipped fruit as soon as possible. Then play one of the following games.

The Mug Game

Go to a secondhand store or antique shop to find mugs or glasses that represent the people in your group. Just don't make it so obvious that everyone will know exactly which mug would go with which person. And don't pay much for these. Tape each person's name inside the mug that represents him or her.

Hand out paper and pencils. Have group members write number one, two, three, etc. for each mug. Then hold up each one and ask who this mug describes. There will be laughter, but ask people to refrain from blurting out names. Also, don't poke fun of anyone if the group is not bonded enough to handle it. When you've gone through them all, go back and ask, "Okay who owns mug number one, two, etc?" Have them tally up their scores to see who wins. Give the winner the gag-gift and give the mugs to the people they described.

The Spice of Our Lives

Raid somebody's spice rack for several jars of various strong-smelling spices. We recommend a mixture of sweet spices: cloves, all-spice, ginger, and cinnamon; and savory ones: dill, sage, thyme, or oregano. Not pepper!

Hold the spices up so that people can see this is not a trick, but you might want to hide the labels. Blindfold contestants one at a time for the scent test. See if they can distinguish some of the similar-smelling spices such as cinnamon and all-spice, or thyme and oregano. Award a prize to the one(s) who guess them all correctly.

Say something like: **Variety, as they say, is the spice of life. Each of us is unique and we each add our own particular spice to life, and certainly to this Bible study group. That's what this party is all about—to celebrate who we are, and especially to celebrate the creative God who made us and who recognizes each of us by the fragrance of our lives.**

 ## Opening

Sing the Doxology ("Praise God from Whom All Blessings Flow") or a chorus such as "He Who Began a Good Work In You." Or, have an expressive reader or recite the poem by Gerard Manley Hopkins, "Pied Beauty" from page 84 of the journal. Then join hands in a circle and have each person call out one thing to praise God for.

2 Bible Study

 ## Focus

Have the Bible study questions rehearsed and memorized if possible. Don't let the study, prayer, singing, or affirmation seem tacked on to the party, they *are* the party. Notice in Luke 7:36-50 that Jesus turned an ordinary party into a life-changing and eternal party, if you will, for this known prostitute.

These past four weeks we have learned a lot about ourselves. We have looked at our personalities, strengths and weaknesses, gifts, and aspirations. Some of us have for the first time discovered that God is the source of all life. Some of us are realizing what Paul meant when he said "In him we live and move and have our being" (Acts 17:28).

• What have you discovered about God and yourself? Is there anything you're still puzzled about?

• Why do people celebrate? What do they usually celebrate? How do you know that a party or celebration will occur?

• What's the best celebration or party you've ever attended? What was unique about it?

Dig In

Luke 24 is the story of Christ's resurrection. In a way, the whole chapter is one gigantic party as Jesus appears to various people after His resurrection. Luke writes it almost like a play in three acts with an epilogue. If your group is up for it, do the Bible study as a pantomime in three acts. Divide into three groups assigning one of the three passages below to each. They are to read through the passage, quickly decide how they are going to pantomime it, and come back together to act each one out in turn followed by the discussion questions.

How it will work is that one person reads the passage as the action is going on. Each group should decide what the climax of that scene is, and if they think it will work, freeze the action at that spot as reader continues the reading. When the reading is completed, the actors dissolve the action and return to their seats for the discussion.

Act One: The Women at the Empty Tomb

Luke 24:1-12. Read over the passage in your group and decide how you will act it out. Then discuss the following questions as a whole group.

• **What invitations do you see in verses 1-12?**

• **Who took the invitation to check out the empty tomb?**

Act Two: On the Road to Emmaus

Luke 24:13-35. Read over the passage in your group and decide how you will act it out. Then discuss the following questions as a whole group.

• **What invitations are there in verses 13-33?** (There are at least four.)

• **In verses 33-35 there is information about people having seen the risen Jesus. Would such information spark your interest? How would**

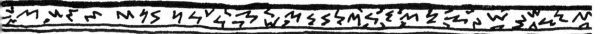

you have explained what happened?

• What invitation is being offered to the hearers in verses 33, 34?

Act Three: Jesus Appears to the Disciples

Luke 24:36-49. Read over the passage in your group and decide how you will act it out. Then discuss the following questions as a whole group.

• Verses 36-49 show Jesus on the scene. What's the atmosphere like now?

• What does His presence prove about physical death?

• What does He say His death and resurrection are about?

• What kinds of invitations does Jesus offer here?

Epilogue: Jesus Ascends to Heaven

Luke 24:50-53. For this section you just need a reader and someone to play the part of Jesus blessing the disciples. You will all be the disciples in the crowd that day. (For the Ascension, perhaps have the person playing Jesus standing on a stair step and slowly walking backwards up the stairs and out of sight, or standing in a doorway, etc.) Finish your discussion with the following questions.

• If death has no hold over Jesus, then how long do His invitations last?

• In verses 52 and 53, what was the response to Jesus' offer on the part of those who saw Him risen?

• What is your response to His claims and invitations?

 ## Reflect and Respond

Close with this thought: **Have you ever thought of Jesus as a party maker, mixer or goer? One of Jesus' invitations is to an eternal party. Have you accepted the invitation?**

Allow time for personal reflection and silent prayer.

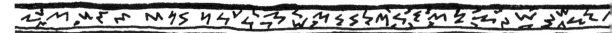

Leadership Tip

You may at this point have someone who wants to respond to Jesus' gift of forgiveness, new, and eternal life. Be prepared for the Holy Spirit to make this happen. Have a party if it does because Heaven will be partying! If more clarification is needed go to Luke 7:36-50 or John 3 and 4.

3 Sharing and Prayer

Now's the time for affirmation and applause. Here you can put the spotlight on one person at a time. For instance, have people tell what they did for the Reaction section of their journals. Let this be a time of general affirmation for everyone.

 I am what I am and that's all that I am. —Popeye, "The Popeye Show"

Ideas: Praise God for creating you by composing your own psalm (perhaps you could set it to music). Tape a picture of yourself on this page and write a description of your unique qualities and abilities.

Go back and share some of the answers to prayer you have seen as a group, as well as those things that need continued prayer.

The true reason we can celebrate both now and in eternity is because of Whose we are. Luke 24 reminds us that, when we are in right relationship with God through Jesus' death on our behalf and living in His resurrection life, applause, adoration and praise are most appropriate. Do it up big in praise to Him. He has done it up big for you!

Have a general cheer for God, then turn up the music and party on.

UNIT Three

I'm Not Alone

Exploring My Connection with Others

"No man is an Island," wrote English poet and Anglican priest, John Donne. "We are all a piece of the continent, a part of the main." One of the most serious problems of our day is the isolation we feel as a result of our individualistic culture. In the sixties and seventies people used to talk about their need to "find themselves." Many homes and lives were shattered as people just walked away from commitments, ties, and responsibilities in their search for personal fulfillment. Today we are reaping the harvest of this imbalance and realizing that nobody's search for identity takes place in a vacuum. Fulfillment and contentment in life are found in the process of meeting responsibilities and in keeping commitments.

Each of us is a member of many groups, family, school, neighborhood, race, nationality, culture, etc. The church was forged by God as the one institution on the face of the earth where all could belong, no matter what race, history, or culture. The unity of the church is in what Christ did on the cross, which transcends all other divisions. Christians are the family of God. But living together is not so easy. This unit explores the meaning and importance of community, and of the things that threaten and build genuine Christian community.

About the author: Kelly Peavey is a former school teacher and free-lance writer in Plaistow, New Hampshire. She and her husband have two children and are active in their church where Kelly has discipled many young women in the Christian faith.

WEEK 11 No Man Is an Island

Theme: God created us for relationships with each other and with Him.

Scripture: Ephesians 2:11-22

1 Getting Started

Housekeeping

Welcome everyone to the Bible study. Introduce any new folks and make brief announcements. You've got five weeks together to talk about and deal with issues of community. Be thinking of something you can do to wrap up this series where you can spend extended time together and actually live through some of what you're talking about. See Week Thirteen for a couple ideas.

Icebreaker

Choose one of the following options or use another activity of your own that illustrates the theme of this week's study.

We're in This Together

Hand out paper and pencils. Have people make a list of everyone they came in contact with today. For example, a bus driver, gas station atten-

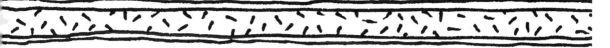

dant, grocery checker, etc. After everyone has a list, have each one go back and jot down what would have happened if these people had not been there. (A gas station without employees means no gas—you can't get very far!)

Now ask them, **What conclusions did you come to about the value of the people you came in contact with today? Could you have made it through the day without them? Explain.**

Of course there will be a few interactions that group members could have done without. Yet, overall they will have to admit that we live in a world where we need each other—whether we like it or not.

I'll Just Do It Myself!

Set the stage for some personal reflection by taking members back to their childhoods with the following scenario. **As a child there must have been at least one time when you wanted to run away and live by yourself, away from all the hassles of living with parents, brothers and sisters, bullies, etc. Even now you probably can think of a time or situation where you felt it would be easier to live a solitary existence on a tropical island rather than deal with _____ .**

Then go around the room and have people share briefly what makes them want to get away from the rest of the world. It may help people feel more comfortable sharing if they write their thoughts first.

Discuss some drawbacks to truly cutting yourself off from the world and doing everything yourself.

For one thing, it would be downright lonely. For another, some things would be impossible. Apart from the members who claim they can live in the wilderness wearing animal skins and eating from the wild, you'll discover as a group that people need people.

Opening

Sing, or play a recording of, the old rock classic "Lean on Me" if you know it. Then ask someone to open in prayer, possibly using something from the prayer they wrote in the Response section of their journals.

2 Bible Study

Focus

Ask members to discuss the diagrams they filled out in the Reflection section of their journals for this week.

Everyone is a member of a number of groups: family, neighborhood, school, nation, human race, etc. Fill in your relationship network, starting with those closest to you emotionally. Any gaps?

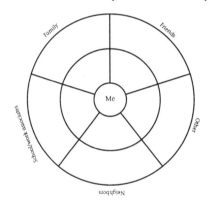

• **What do you think of when you hear the word "community"?**

You'll probably get responses related to where people live, i.e., people living together, the people in a neighborhood, etc. Some may point out that we also use the word to talk about any group of people who are united by some common interest, concern, or circumstance, such as the "black community," the "gay community," the "Christian community," etc. If you have a dictionary handy, read the definitions.

• **Which circle on your diagram comprises your "community"?**

• **What makes a community a community?**

In the New Testament, the church existed as a community. The common life that the believers lived was more than just a cookies-and-punch kind of "fellowship." Our studies these next five weeks are all about what makes a community a genuine community.

Dig In

Have someone read Ephesians 2:11-22. Explain that the early church, like the church today, struggled with diversity—especially between Jews and Gentiles. Ask members to consider the differences mentioned between Jew and Gentile. You may want to guide them with questions like these:

• **How did the Gentiles, or the "uncircumcised," differ from the Jews, the "circumcised"?**

Jot down group members' responses on a large sheet of paper or poster board, or have members make their own lists.

Here are some of the things they may come up with:

The Gentiles were

   • separate from Christ

   • excluded from citizenship in Israel

   • foreigners to the covenants of the promise

   • without hope

   • without God

• **In what ways were you, or are you, like the Gentiles described in verses 11 and 12?**

If you think members would be more comfortable sharing this in smaller groups, have them divide into groups of 2-3. After a few minutes, come back and discuss their answers. Focus on general feelings and thoughts, rather than specifics of members' lives that may make them uncomfortable.

No matter what our background, it all comes down to this: We are all separated from God apart from Christ. Without Jesus we have no claims to God's promises, no hope, and no relationship with our Creator.

But God had a plan to reconcile and rescue us from our desperate situation. Read verses 13-22.

• **How were the Gentiles brought near to God?**

• **What does it mean that He abolished in Christ's flesh the law with its**

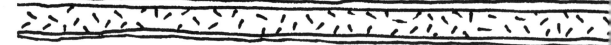

commandments and regulations? Does that mean that we no longer have to keep the Ten Commandments?

People may need some help here. See the Inside Insights.

• **At any rate, what does verse 15 say was God's purpose?**

• **What did Jesus' death on the cross provide for the Jews?**

There are at least three things according to this passage: reconciliation to God (vs. 16); peace (vss. 14 and 17); and access by the Holy Spirit (vs. 18).

Paul especially stresses that Christ's death on the cross reconciled both Jew and Gentile to God. This was tough to swallow for the early church because of the cultural gap and prejudices between Jews and Gentiles.

• **In verses 19-22 what does Paul mean when he describes the Gentiles as "members of God's household?"**

When you think of a member of a household, you might think of a husband, wife, brother, or sister. Paul is also speaking of a physical building with Christ as the cornerstone. The foundation is made up of apostles and prophets. Pretty prestigious company, huh?

INSIDE

■ Matthew 5:17 and Romans 3:31 teach that God's moral standards were not changed by the coming of Christ. So "abolishing in his flesh the law with its commandments and regulations" cannot mean that the Ten Commandments no longer apply. There are two possibilities: (1) It could mean the kinds of specific regulations, such as the dietary laws, etc., that made Jews ritually pure and kept Gentiles at a distance. Or, (2) It could mean that Jesus abolished the Law by fulfilling it when He took upon Himself the penalty for breaking the commandments—death—even though He Himself did not break any of them.

Next, have members break into groups of 2 or 3. Give each group a large sheet of paper and a marker. Have someone read verses 19-22 aloud. Then ask each group to draw a picture of these verses. Encourage them to draw themselves somewhere in the picture, even those who may not yet be a member of God's household. They could show themselves coming close to investigate.

After a few minutes, have each group show their picture and describe it to the group. Where are they in the picture and why did they place themselves in that particular place?

Reflect and Respond

Wrap up your study by having members reflect on a few questions that bring the Scripture home to them.

• **How would you describe what God has done to bring people into a relationship with Himself and others?**

• **What is the value of being in relationship with God through Jesus Christ?**

Allow members to share their responses and insights from the study and their journals at this time.

3 Sharing and Prayer

This is a time for sharing personal concerns and prayer requests. Allow at least 10 minutes for prayer.

You may want to divide into groups of 3-4 to encourage community among group members. Be sensitive to newcomers and nonbelievers in your group.

If you'd like, close by singing a song such as "Give Thanks," or by reading Ephesians 2:19-22 in unison. Both affirm membership in God's family and His plan to bind Christians together in relationship to Him through Christ.

We're in This Together

Theme: What it means to be part of a body.

Scripture: I Corinthians 12:12—13:13

1 Getting Started

Housekeeping

Welcome everyone and briefly make necessary announcements.

Icebreaker

With One Arm Tied Behind My Back

The most simple tasks become complex with one arm tied behind your back. But it's possible to get things done with the help of a friend or two. This activity is designed to promote teamwork.

Break members up into groups of 3-4 and have everyone tie one arm behind his or her back. (A bandana or sock tied around the wrist through a belt loop works well.) Then have a race to see which group can complete the following tasks first. Set an egg timer for five minutes to prevent the activity from going too long. Go over the tasks quickly and answer any questions. Give each group a copy of the following list or write the list on a large piece of paper or writing board.

Tasks (add to, or take away from, this list depending on what you have available to work with):

- make a peanut butter and jelly sandwich
- take off the shoe and sock of one member
- untie and tie a member's shoelace
- unbutton and button three buttons on a member's shirt or sweater
- thread a needle
- peel a banana
- sharpen a pencil

After the craziness, discuss what was difficult about completing the tasks. What was the hardest task? Why is it so hard to work together?

Opening

Sing something like "They'll Know We Are Christians by Our Love." Then ask someone to open in prayer, possibly using something from the prayer he or she wrote in the Response section of the journals.

2 Bible Study

Focus

Have group members think about what part of the body best describes them and why. Would they be a mouth because they talk a lot? A leg because they are always on the run? You get the idea. Then see what kind of a body you end up with. On a large sheet of paper or writing board, have people come up and draw the parts of the body they picked to describe themselves. Don't forget to have members explain why

they selected a particular part. (Obviously there is the potential for some raw humor here. See I Corinthians 12:23 for how Paul treated this subject.)

Wrap up the activity by discussing what kind of body you make as a group.

• **What essential parts are lacking? Are there any parts that you have too many of?**

• **What about the parts not selected? Did anyone choose the stomach, back, or eardrum? Why do you think these parts were overlooked?**

Dig In

Have the group turn to I Corinthians 12:12—13:13. Since this passage of Scripture is about the body of Christ, you may want to read I Corinthians 12:12-31a, the first section of Scripture, in unison. It's lengthy, but reading it as one will be a wonderful object lesson. Stop reading at "But eagerly desire the greater gifts." You will pick up the last sentence in chapter 12 and all of chapter 13 later.

After reading in unison, open the study by having members discuss how the body of Christ, the church, is compared to a body in the passage. You may want to spur discussion with the following questions.

• **Why does Paul compare the church with a body? Is this a good metaphor? Why?**

• **What does Paul use to illustrate each person's uniqueness in the body?**

In examining our physical body and applying the same concept to the church, Paul shows the need for diversity. Just because one person does not have the talents and traits of another does not mean he or she is not needed in the body. Often we want to put limits and requirements on the way people should be and act within the church. Paul stresses that God has made us each different, and for good reason. A body of eyes wouldn't get very far. Likewise, a body of feet couldn't see where it was going. But when we combine all the various personalities, talents, and abilities God has given His people, we have a complete body.

• **What does Paul say Christians should do to prevent division in the body?**

The key here is honor and respect. All parts are honorable. Though some

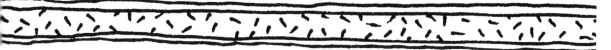

may seem weak or unpresentable, they are not less valuable. Members of the body should have concern for one another, supporting and caring for one another.

- **Is this how you see Christians treating each other in the church?**

- **Is this how you treat others?**

Allow some time for members to really think about this one. You may have a few moments of silence while members take on the uncomfortable task of examining themselves. Don't let that throw you. After a moment, ask people to share what they could do differently to support and encourage each other in the small group.

If you have a writing board handy, jot down people's comments.

At this point, finish reading the passage, I Corinthians 12:31b–13:13. Using the Scripture passage as a guide, list the qualities of love beside the suggestions you came up with from the previous question. Note which qualities you already had listed on your own. What new qualities stand out to you?

- **According to this description of love, describe in your own words what it means to love.**

Of the many qualities described in chapter 13, a general principle that stands out is that love thinks of others first. Unlike the world's view of "Looking out for number one," love looks out for others. In a world where everyone is screaming out for their "rights," love denies its rights if necessary and offers generosity and forgiveness.

Have someone reread I Corinthians 13:9-13 out loud.

- **What do you think it means to see "face to face" and to "know fully, even as I am fully known"?** (See next page.)

Just as a child grows into adulthood, Christians grow spiritually from infants to adults. That's encouraging. Plus, the Bible tells us that believers will know God fully—even as He knows us fully.

- **Why do you think it was necessary for Paul to go into such great detail about the unity of the body? Is this emphasis still needed today?**

- **How does the definition of love fit into the goal of unity in the church?**

Reflect and Respond

At this point, discuss the two questions on page 106 of the journal. The second question may be particularly good for seekers who are looking at Christians and the church to see if what we say is really true.

How do you explain the difference between the ideal of unity in the body of Christ with the reality you see around you among Christians and different churches?

If unity among Christians were more of a reality, what would that look like, and what would it say to you? Why?

INSIDE

■ The word "perfection" can mean "completeness," "fulfillment," or "maturity." The perfection to come in I Corinthians 13:9-13 most likely refers to Christ's return. Some scholars interpret it to mean the completion of the written revelation of God in Scripture. Others take it to mean the maturity or establishment of the church. But verse 12 seems to indicate that Paul is referring to the Second Coming because only when Christ returns will we finally understand everything and "know fully even as [we are] known."

3 Sharing and Prayer

During this time allow people to share personal concerns. Then break into groups or prayer partners for prayer. Close by joining hands in prayer for the unity of the church and of your group.

Community Matters

Theme: The importance of community.

Scripture: Acts 2:42-47

1 Getting Started

Housekeeping

With only two weeks (meetings) left to go after today, you'll need to start thinking of whether or not you're going to continue meeting as a group, and if so, what you're going to do next. Of course we'd suggest something else in the Discovery Series or the Great Groups line—perhaps a Bible study book from the Good Word series. Whatever you decide, you should plan to have another kind of social activity together to provide closure to this study. Discuss ideas together and get people thinking about it for next week.

Depending on the time of year, you might want to take a bike trip or a weekend camping trip together. (Separate tents for guys and gals, of course, and a chaperone if some are under 18 is essential.) But the extended time together will be a bonding experience and also force you to work through some community issues. If you do go away together, you might want to do the last session on your trip.

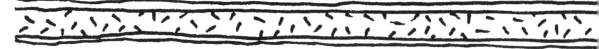

 ## Icebreaker

Choose one of the following activities or create one of your own.

Esteem Builders

This activity will work best if members know each other, even if it is just a little bit. Have members write their names at the top of a sheet of paper. Then tape each person's paper on his or her back. Now, have members go around and write positive things they have noticed about the person on his or her paper. This can be anything from "I love your purple shoes" to "You are very kind and friendly."

After 3-5 minutes people can take their papers from their backs and read them. Discuss how the positive feedback makes them feel. Everyone likes to be encouraged and to hear positive things about him/herself. There is so much to tear us down—a bad test grade, a critical classmate, or an irritable boss, and so on. We all need a safe place where we can go to be built up. The church is supposed to be that kind of place.

Gift Giving

Living in community requires patience, tolerance, and generosity. Invite people to share a time when they gave an extraordinary gift or shared their most prize possession.

• **What compelled you to do such a thing?**

• **Were the results what you expected?**

Most likely, some will tell a warm tale of sacrifice, giving, and joyful acceptance. However, there may be someone whose gift backfired. (If not, bring up the possibility of an unappreciated gift.)

• **What motivates someone to accept or reject a gift?**

The most pure motivation for giving is rooted in love. Jesus said to love God with all your heart, soul, and mind, and to love your neighbor as yourself. This is difficult to do and often our actions don't bring the results we imagine. Still, the response of others does not add to or take away from the value of the gift. Our actions are a picture of our love for one another and for God.

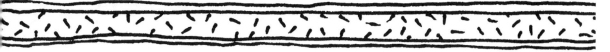

The way we act toward one another in the church says a lot about our relationship with God. The Bible says if we truly love Him, we will love one another.

Opening

Sing "Behold What Manner Of Love," or "They'll Know We Are Christians by Our Love." Then ask someone to open in prayer.

2 Bible Study

Focus

Before the study select two people for the following two role-plays.

#1

Person A (runs in frantically): My car won't start and I'm late for work!

Person B (reading a book, responding without looking up): Oh, really? What's wrong with it?

Person A: I don't know, but I can't be late again. I'll get fired. I hate my car!

Person B (still not looking up): I'd hate it too if it made me late to work every day.

Person A: Can you help me? Could you take me to work?

Person B (sigh): I really wanted to read. I guess I could take you in a couple of hours if you can't get a ride from someone else. I wanted to go to the mall later anyway.

Ask people to give their thoughts about the characters. What did the mannerisms and words say about each? Most likely they'll say Person B was selfish, insensitive, and uncaring. They will probably sympathize with Person A's need and wonder why Person B didn't help.

The next role-play shows how this scenario might play out differently.

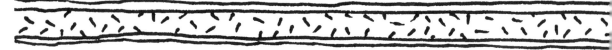

#2 .

Person A (runs in frantically): My car won't start and I'm late for work!

Person B (reading a book, puts down the book): Oh, really? What's wrong with it?

Person A: I don't know, but I can't be late again. I'll get fired. I hate my car!

Person B: You sound really frustrated. Is there anything I can do?

Person A: Could you take me to work?

Person B: Why don't you just take my car? That way you'll have a ride home too.

• How do you react to Person B now? What does his willingness to go beyond the request for a ride and offering up his car say about his character?

The way we act toward others says a lot about who we are.

When the Christian church came into existence at Pentecost, and in her earliest days, the people gave evidence of the reality of the presence of God in their midst. As an outgrowth of that, they gave generously, and God was glorified in their actions.

 Dig In

Have a member read the Scripture passage, Acts 2:42-47. Ask the group to react to the description of the earliest days of the Christian church. There is much that stands out as different from our inter-actions within the church today. You can leave the discussion open or explore the group's responses to questions like these.

• What were believers devoted to in these early days of the church's existence? What were the results of their devotion?

You may want to explore what it means to be devoted to someone or some-thing before getting into the answers to this question. In our culture, the word "devoted" is used most often to describe romantic love. In this pas-sage of Scripture, devotion describes the church's sincere desire to learn about God and to be together. Within this environment of love and support many miraculous signs and wonders were performed.

• Describe how the believers interacted with each other. What do their

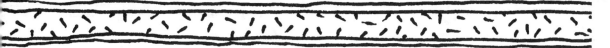

actions say about how they felt about each other?

If you have a writing board you could write the actions on one side and what those actions convey on the other side. For example, all believers were together—this shows commitment, harmony, and companionship. Other actions include having everything in common, selling their possessions, giving to those in need, meeting every day at the temple, breaking bread together, praising God, enjoying each other's favor.

• **Compare the actions of the early church to the church today. What is similar and what is different?**

• **The believers are described as glad, sincere, and full of praise. Is this how you would describe yourself or the Christians you know?**

• **Do you think the church today could support each other the way the early church did?**

Discuss the pros and cons of this kind of a lifestyle. In reality, these actions were not any easier two thousand years ago. It is only by the Holy Spirit that we are able to give sincerely, joyfully, and sacrificially day in and day out. This is a good time to emphasize that selling everything is not the emphasis of this passage. Though this act, when properly motivated, is honorable to God, it is not the focus. The central theme in this passage is the church's devotion to God and each other. Out of this devotion came all of their actions. (See next page.)

• **What does this passage say God was doing all this time? Is there a connection?**

Verse 47 says He added to their numbers daily.

• **Why would people be attracted to Christ when observing the early church?**

• **How do you think the early believers would define the body of Christ?**

 ## Reflect and Respond

Close the study with a few questions for personal reflection and application.

• **What stands out to you most about the early church?**

If there are seekers or new Christians in your group, ask what attracts or

■ Many people think that this passage describes an early form of communism. While there are certainly similarities between the ideals of communism and what is described here, there are also important differences. It was not an ideology that compelled the early Christians; it was their love for Christ. And, even in the early church, people had private property (see 4:36). It's just that they considered their rights to private property or privacy as less important than the needs of their brothers and sisters. Their motivation was internal, not external, or controlled by a central bureaucracy.

Many groups down through history, Christian and non-Christian, have tried communal living. More often than not, even in Christian groups, these experiments in social engineering have resulted in failure, with a few notable exceptions.

The monastic movements in the Catholic tradition were reform movements that sought to pattern themselves on the example of the early believers. Today, there are Christians who are trying to live out this lifestyle, not by living together in a commune, but by reclaiming the concept of the church in a neighborhood—where anyone who has a need can be cared for.

first attracted them to Christianity. Do they see this kind of community and love among the Christians they know (including the rest of you)?

If everyone is a Christian in your group, ask if they think others would be attracted to God when they view your Christian community? Why or why not?

Allow members to respond to these questions or share thoughts from page 114 of their journals.

 What would you expect it to be like if God were actually present with a group of people? Have you ever experienced such a thing? If so, describe it. If not, why do you think you haven't? Would you want to?

3 Sharing and Prayer

Encourage people to praise God in their prayers as the early believers did. Close by saying the Lord's Prayer in unison. If people don't know it, it's Matthew 6:9-13.

Community Dangers

Theme: Things that threaten community.

Scripture: Acts 5:1-14; 6:1-7; Galatians 5:13-26

1 Getting Started

Housekeeping

Make any announcements necessary regarding your plans for closure to this study series.

Icebreaker

Choose one of the following activities or use one of your own that illustrates this week's theme.

Party Poopers

Have members break up into pairs. One will play the part of the party goer and the other will play the part of the party pooper. The object is for the party goer to try to convince the party pooper to go to the party. The party pooper is to make excuses for not going to the party.

After a few minutes, stop and discuss some of the reasons to go to the party and excuses not to go. How did they feel playing their roles? In most cases, the party pooper will feel negative or apathetic. Some members may also feel a sense of power in being negative. The party goer will probably feel frustrated and possibly even angry.

This party illustration is a lot like going to church. There will always be plenty of excuses not to go. Being part of the body is not a spectator sport; you have to get involved. No matter what your excuse, you can't enjoy the party unless you attend. And in the church, Jesus is the guest of honor at the party. Is there an excuse valid enough to miss celebrating with the King of Kings?

Attitude Check

On a sheet of paper make two lists.

In List 1 write negative phrases like the following:

It will never work
It's not my fault
I hate that
It's not my problem
I'm too busy
We've already tried that
I don't want to
That's not my responsibility
What a waste of time
Impossible

In List 2 write positive phrases such as:

Let's try it
I'll help
I'd like to
Let me work with you
Sure
I have time
Okay
No problem
Good idea
Way to go

Make enough copies of the paper for the group. Pass out the sheet and have members select one phrase from List 1. Now ask them to walk around the room saying that phrase and nothing else to others in the group. It will be like a crazy cocktail party with everyone saying the same thing over and over again. After a few minutes have them pick a phrase from List 2 and do the same thing.

It's a silly way for the group to see the destructive and constructive effects of the way we speak to one another. Talk briefly about how they felt speaking and hearing the phrases in each list.

Opening

Open by singing some group favorites, or perhaps the Scripture song based on I John 4:7, 8, "Beloved, Let Us Love One Another." Then ask someone to open in prayer.

2 Bible Study

Focus

Ask group members to discuss their insights from the Scripture Discovery section of their journals on what causes conflicts and divisions in the church. Then discuss how we can explain the contrast between the kind of community we read about in the early church last week and what we see around us among Christians today. Is real community possible?

Today's study is going to examine how that initial community began to break down and how the church responded to the problems they began to face.

Dig In

You'll be looking at two short sections in the book of Acts to follow up on last week's narrative, then examine a section of a letter from Paul to the church at Galatia in which he discusses some things that threaten unity in the body of Christ.

First look up the story of Ananias and Sapphira. Read Acts 5:1-14.

• **How is the picture here different than what we saw last week among the early believers?**

• **What was Ananias's sin?**

Make sure people realize that the problem was not that Ananias kept back part of the sale of his property. That was his right. It was that he lied. His motive was not generosity; it was to look good.

You could spend a whole hour discussing people's reactions to the severity of God's judgment against Ananias, but that's not the main point of this study, so be careful not to get sidetracked on this. Allow people to hold their own opinions, but draw their attention to the results of what happened on the believers and on other people.

• **What kind of effect did the church at this stage of its life have on the people around them? See verses 12-14. What elements contributed to their impact?**

You'll probably note both the fear that the experience with Ananias and Sapphira generated, as well as the impact of the miracles the apostles performed.

Leader's Tip

You may have skeptics in your group who question the believability of this account. That's okay. Remind them, however, of the rules of the inductive method. Let the text speak for itself. There may be some who would speculate about the situation with Ananias and Sapphira. Did God really strike them dead, or was there foul play and the story was made up to cover it up and strike fear into people's hearts?

This is the way we are conditioned to think about the things we read in our newspapers, etc. If something like this is suggested, don't be threatened by it. You may want to simply say that this book is a primary document, written by an eyewitness, and thus has strong historical validity. We were not there, so any other explanation is pure speculation. This is what the text says. We must take it at face value and ask, if this is what really happened, what would the results have been? Is it internally consistent?

Now turn to a story that's much easier to relate to. Read Acts 6:1-7.

• **What is the situation here? What would we call this problem today?**

Racial or ethnic discrimination.

• **What do you think of the way they solved it? What did it show about the kind of community they had?**

There are probably several things people might note. One is that there was a division of leadership. The twelve apostles definitely were in charge, but it was a communal decision to which they all agreed. This is also the first time in Acts we see the idea of a division of labor, with priority given to the ministry of the Word (study, teaching, and preaching) and of prayer.

• **What kind of qualifications did these new "waiters" have to have? Why were these qualities so important?**

Note that they were all spiritual, internal qualifications. The job may have been manual, but their character was considered most important. You may also want to point out that all of these names are Greek, so that they would probably be more sensitive to the needs of this minority population in Jerusalem. (A case of First-Century Affirmative Action?)

• **What was the result of this decision?**

Again, the result was that the Word of God spread and many more people, including Jewish priests, were converted.

You've looked at two stories in which something threatened the young Christian community. In both cases, that threat was met and overcome. Summarize what you've observed so far by identifying the things that threatened the new community. Write down what you come up with. Below are some suggestions.

Things that can threaten community:
  • hypocrisy
  • dishonesty
  • prejudice and discrimination
  • lack of concern for the poor and needy
  • lack of organization or a reasonable division of labor
  • allowing leadership to get sidetracked with issues other people could handle, or an overly controlling leadership that does not know how to delegate responsibility, etc.

Now look at a passage from a letter Paul wrote to one of the early churches. This passage gives a summary of things that can threaten, not only community, but also a person's own spirituality. It also gives an explanation for why there are problems in the church, and always have been. Read Galatians 5:16-18.

• **How do these verses apply to what we've been talking about? What does Paul say is the explanation for problems and conflicts that develop among Christians, and within each of us individually?**

Basically, the problem is our sinful natures. Even the early Christians were not perfect. They still struggled with their sinful natures.

Now read Galatians 5:19-21 and have the group list the various acts of the sinful nature along with possible consequences of those acts. For example, sexual immorality = broken relationships.

You could have them divide into groups of 2-3 to do this, or do it together and put your list on a writing board. Take time to discuss your findings and insights on the consequences of sin. There are many negative consequences of sin. One of the biggest consequences of life by the sinful nature is in verse 21, "those who live like this will not inherit the kingdom of God."

• **How does Paul say we can overcome our sinful tendencies?**

Paraphrased—by living in the power of the Holy Spirit. Now read verses 22-26. List the fruit of the Spirit in verses 22, 23 and a possible result for each. For example, love = people feel valued. You may want to do this in small groups as well if you have time.

The Spirit produces fruit in all Christians, according to this passage. There is no requirement to receiving these qualities other than walking in step with, or in tune with the Holy Spirit, who is given to a person when he or she accepts Jesus Christ as Savior.

• **How does the sinful nature affect the body of Christ?**

Try to bring the discussion closer to home by focusing on things that affect each one of us personally, such as gossiping, lying, harboring resentment, etc.

• **How does life by the Spirit affect the church?**

There are many benefits that could be named. In general, life by the Spirit draws the body together, enabling members to draw nearer to each other and to God.

• **How does Paul describe those who belong to Christ? How should they live?**

This passage says that those who belong to Christ no longer live by their sinful nature, but by the Spirit. However, Christians also play an active role in following the leading of the Spirit. It is not like living your life on auto-pilot with the Spirit making all your decisions. Rather, the Spirit is a guide to follow as we study God's Word and spend time in prayer.

Reflect and Respond

Close your study with a couple of questions for personal application and reflection.

• **What aspects of the sinful nature stand out to you as particularly dangerous for the church?**

• **After reading Galatians 5:22-26, do you think any items from these verses describe you?**

Allow people to share insights from the study or their journal at this time, either from the Reaction or Response sections.

In your opinion, what is wrong with the church today? Any constructive ideas for improvement?

If it is possible, as far as it depends on you, live at peace with everyone.

—Romans 12:18

It's easy to point the finger of blame at others for the discord in relationships. The difficulty lies in examining yourself and the areas you need to work on. The problem may not be yours, but you're the only one you can change. Pause a moment and reflect.

◼3 Sharing and Prayer

During this prayer time, have members break into small groups or prayer partners. Allow 5-10 minutes for sharing personal concerns and at least 10 minutes for prayer. Ask members to pray for the protection of the church from sins that bring destruction to the body at some point in their prayer time.

WEEK 15 Building Blocks

Theme: The things that build community.

Scripture: Romans 12:9—13:1

1 Getting Started

Housekeeping

If you are going to get away together on some kind of a retreat, you may need some extra time to take care of last-minute details. Make sure your plans are clear and that everyone knows who's going to do what. You may want to do all or part of this study then.

Icebreaker

Make a Wish

Give each member a piece of paper and a pen. Tell everyone: **Make a list of things you wish you could have. The sky's the limit—a new car, unlimited patience, a trip to Hawaii, etc.**

Set a timer for two minutes so you don't spend too much time on this (most of us could go on wishing forever).

Next, reset the timer for two minutes and this time write a list of things you would give to someone else. Again, the sky's the limit and the gift recipients

can be anyone and everyone—a cordless telephone for my sister, straight A's for my best friend, world peace, etc.

Once you've completed your lists, discuss which list was more fun to create and why. When you view your personal wish list how do you feel? Are you more thankful or less thankful for what you have? When you view your list for others how do you feel?

Often, focusing on what we want causes us to lose sight of what God has already given us. Frustration, disappointment, and selfishness can be the result. On the other hand, when we focus on others and their needs we are filled with love and compassion. Mysteriously, in most cases we feel greater joy and contentment when we are able to joyfully give to others than when we stack up things for ourselves.

Building Basics

You'll need stackable items for this activity—wooden blocks, plastic bowls and cups, cans, books, or whatever. Divide into groups of 3-4. Put building materials in the center of the room. Groups have 4 minutes to build a building. It can be tall, wide, fancy, unique, anything you wish. The only criteria is that it be the best building you can build. You may take building materials as needed, but don't hoard materials. If you have a timer, set it to give a clear indication of when construction begins and ends.

Once buildings are complete, have a spokesperson from each group briefly describe the qualities of their structures. Then discuss general construction principles such as: there must be a firm foundation, materials provide support for each other, some materials stack better than others, there must be a design or plan to keep the building from falling, etc.

• **How did it feel to share building materials? Was it easy? Difficult? Why?**

• **How are these buildings like the church?**

For starters, the church is built on the foundation of Jesus Christ, members support each other, and God has a plan and design for His church, etc.

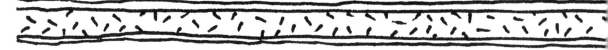

Opening

Sing something about unity in the church, such as "They'll Know We Are Christians by Our Love," or "The Building Block," etc. Ask someone to open in prayer, possibly using the opening quote from this week's journal.

Christian brotherhood is not an ideal which we must realize; it is rather a reality created by God in Christ in which we may participate.

—Dietrich Bonhoeffer, Life Together

Thank God for the unity we have in Christ, and ask His presence with your group as you complete this study. Ask that your study may not be simply a "head" exercise, but that God would bind you together as group in His Spirit, that you may experience genuine Christian community.

2 Bible Study

Focus

Most everyone has had a best friend. Ask people to share how a person becomes a best friend.

The scenario might differ in details, but most everyone will cite some of the following—a common interest or goal, time together in difficulty and in fun, and respect for the person as he or she is. Friendship doesn't happen overnight, and neither does the experience of community within the church. Walking up to someone and saying "be my friend" doesn't usually result in a lasting relationship. In the same way, expecting church members to sacrifice their pride and personal desires in order to agree and work together is not likely to occur from just talking about it. Living in community involves action and commitment.

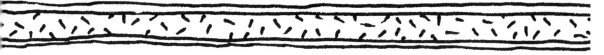

 ## Dig In

Romans 12:9—13:1

In this passage, Paul gives a number of commands for Christian behavior. Since every sentence contains a directive, you may want to go around the room having each person read a verse until you've read the entire passage.

• **This passage is full of "dos" and "don'ts." What are some of them?**
Break into groups of 2-3 for this or work together and write your findings on a writing board or large sheet of paper.

Below is a partial list. Some of these are direct quotes, some are paraphrases, and some are inferences. You can make your list(s) any way you want.

Do	*Don't*
love sincerely	be insincere
hate evil	love evil
cling to what's good	let your zeal fade
be devoted to each other	curse
honor others above yourself	be proud
stay fervent by serving the Lord	be conceited
be joyful in hope	repay anyone evil for evil
patient in affliction	take revenge
faithful in prayer	be overcome by evil
share with those in need	be rebellious against authority
practice hospitality	
bless those who persecute you	
rejoice with those who rejoice	
mourn with those who mourn	
live in harmony with each other	
be willing to associate with outcasts	
be careful to always do what's right	
as much as possible, live at peace with everyone	
leave room for God's wrath	
if your enemy's hungry, feed him, etc.	
overcome evil with good	
submit to governing authorities	

• **Do you think it's possible to follow all the commands on this list? Explain.**

The Bible calls us to "be holy." It says that God has made Christians holy through Jesus. Though believers may still sin and make mistakes, they are to strive to live according to the Spirit of God and follow the commands given in Scripture.

• **Which commands do you think are particularly difficult to obey? Why?**

Allow people to share openly and encourage each other by following up responses with questions like this one, "Does anyone have a suggestion on how to follow that command?" There probably won't be complete solutions to our struggles with sin, but it's good to share what works for us and to encourage each other to do right.

• **Do any of the commands surprise you? Explain.**

You may have some who are surprised by the reference to God getting revenge in verse 19 (after all, God is love), or by the command to submit to government in 13:1. Allow members to express themselves. Then ask if anyone in the group wants to share the benefits of the command.

Another one they may find somewhat pleasantly surprising is verse 18. "If it is possible, as far as it depends on you, live at peace with everyone." This sort of lets us off the hook in a sense. Paul seems to realize that there are some people with whom it is impossible to live at peace. We are responsible for our own problems, but there some people who refuse to do the same, and there's sometimes not a whole lot you can do to get along with them. (See Titus 3:10 for how the church needs to deal with extreme cases.)

• **What do you think Paul was trying to accomplish by giving this list of commands to the Romans?**

• **What would the church be like if Christians followed the commands in this passage of Scripture?**

There is plenty of room for imagination on this one. For starters, the church would be a loving, secure, safe place filled with peace, joy, comfort, and generosity.

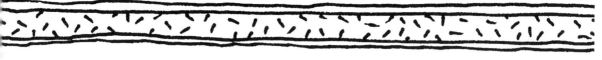

Reflect and Respond

Close your study by having people share how they've grown and changed through this series, and allow them to share insights from their journals. What suggestions do they have for further growth, either for themselves or for your group? You might start with the activity on page 130 of the journals.

Draw a cartoon, write a dialogue or somehow creatively express how you've come to feel about the church.

• **What can we do to develop community in this group?**

3 Sharing and Prayer

Let this be a celebration time. Be sure to discuss current, and ongoing, prayer concerns, and also the ways you've seen God work through your prayers these last five weeks.

If there are still individuals who have not yet made a commitment to Christ, ask them where they're at. Are they one step closer, still confused, still skeptical? Or is there something blocking their understanding or submission to Christ? Be sensitive about this, of course, but don't let the opportunity go by to challenge a person under conviction of the Holy Spirit to take a step of faith.

If there is someone who has come to know Christ through this study, ask how he or she has grown and how your group can continue to help. If, for some reason, you are not going to continue as a group, make sure to get any new Christians hooked up with a prayer partner and one or two people to follow up on discipling them. (You might want to start a discipleship group using one of the books in the Main Thing series if the person is ready.)